THE PARATROOPERS OF THE FRENCH FOREIGN LEGION

—◦◦◦—

From Vietnam to Bosnia

THE PARATROOPERS OF THE FRENCH FOREIGN LEGION

From Vietnam to Bosnia

by

HOWARD R. SIMPSON

BRASSEY'S

Washington • *London*

Copyright © 1997 by Howard R. Simpson

Brassey's Editorial Offices:	Brassey's Order Department:
22883 Quicksilver Drive	P.O. Box 960
Dulles, Virginia 20186	Herndon, Virginia 20172

Brassey's books are available at special discounts for bulk purchases for sales promotions, premiums, fund-raising, or educational use.

Library of Congress Cataloging-in-Publication Data

Simpson, Howard R., 1925–
    The paratroopers of the French Foreign Legion : from Vietnam to Bosnia / by Howard R. Simpson.
        p.   cm.
    Includes index.
    ISBN 1-57488-117-5 (hardcover)
    1. France. Armée. Légion étrangère. Régiment ètranger de parachutistes, 2e—History. 2. France—History, Military.
I. Title.
UD485.F7S56   1997
356'.166'0944—dc21   96-50414
                                                      CIP

Typeset by Graphic Composition, Inc.

First Edition
10 9 8 7 6 5 4 3 2 1

Printed in the United States of America

To my grandchildren,
so they might understand the times we lived in.

 # An AUSA Institute of Land Warfare Book

The Association of the United States Army, or AUSA, was founded in 1950 as a nonprofit organization dedicated to education concerning the role of the U.S. Army, to providing material for military professional development, and to the promotion of proper recognition and appreciation of the profession of arms. Its constituencies include those who serve in the Army today, including Army National Guard, Army Reserve, and Army civilians, the retirees and veterans who have served in the past, and all their families. A large number of public-minded citizens and business leaders are also an important constituency. The association seeks to educate the public, elected and appointed officials, and leaders of the defense industry on crucial issues involving the adequacy of our national defense, particularly those issues affecting land warfare.

In 1988, AUSA established within its existing organization a new entity known as the Institute of Land Warfare. ILW's mission is to extend the educational work of AUSA by sponsoring a wide range of publications, to include books, monographs, and essays on key defense issues, as well as workshops, symposia, and since 1992, a television series. Among the volumes chosen as "An AUSA Institute of Land Warfare Book" are both new texts and reprints of titles of enduring value. Topics include history, policy issues, strategy, and tactics. Publication as an AUSA Book does not indicate that the Association of the United States Army and the publisher agree with everything in the book but does suggest that AUSA and the publisher believe the book will stimulate the thinking of AUSA members and others concerned about important defense-related issues.

CONTENTS

PREFACE

I initially encountered the French Foreign Legion during the hot summer of 1945 in Marseille. Along with other American veterans of the European campaign, I was waiting for a troop ship that would take us halfway around the world for the invasion of the Japanese Home Islands. We considered ourselves a tough, cynical bunch, about as close to real soldiers as any draftees could be. But the arrival of the Foreign Legion in the bars along the Canebière took the edge off any temptation on our part for vainglorious posturing as liberators and victors.

We had been impressed by the tough, tanned, often bearded Legionnaires, their arms traced with elaborate tattoos. For many of these professionals, the war had begun in 1939. Along with the rest of the French Army, they had experienced defeat and a period of confused loyalties until de Gaulle's Free French forces once again entered the war on the side of the Allies. The Legion had then fought its way from the deserts of North Africa through Italy and southern France and into Germany.

Patrolling American MPs warned us that these seemingly taciturn soldiers, wearing the distinctive black visored white cap, the *képi blanc*, were as adept at barroom brawls as they were in actual combat. This proved only too true, and the lesson was learned the hard way by some GIs who insisted on testing the theory.

Today, except for military buffs, the non-French public is generally unaware that the French Foreign Legion still exists. In popular imagination, the Legion occupies a vague niche of memory linked to successive screen adaptations of P. C. Wren's *Beau Geste* and other less imaginative adventure novels. The Legion's public image remains that of Legionnaires in heavy blue coats and white képis, fitted with sun protective neck flaps, laboring over the sand dunes laden with packs, sausage roll blankets, long Lebel rifles, pigsticker bayonets, and rattling mess gear.

To some, the Legion still has the romantic ring of exotic adventure in a man's world where the sun is hot, the intermittent combat victorious, and the cool desert evenings filled with passable wine and compliant females. To others, the Legion is a negative, outdated organization conjuring up colonial conquest, oppressive brutality, and the mercenary profession.

The Legion has been dogged by such extremes of perception since its founding in 1831. In March of that year, King Louis-Philippe of France, eager to clear his nation of an influx of foreigners and provide a fighting force for France's colonial campaigns, issued a royal ordinance. Article I of the ordinance called for the formation of a "legion composed of foreigners" and stipulated that this legion would bear the name "Légion Étrangère," or Foreign Legion. Today, continued misconceptions about the Legion are shared by Walter Mitty dreamers and antimilitary critics alike. Both have missed the point. The contemporary Legion of foreigners is simply an efficient fighting unit of the French Army implementing the orders of the French government, whether of the Right or Left. This mobile fighting force of 8,500 professional soldiers and 350 officers is ready for action anywhere in the world on extremely short notice. Also, unlike other units of the French Army, the Legion has no young civilian recruits in its ranks doing their compulsory military service. Thus, the French government does not have to worry about political or parental opposition to rapid overseas deployment.

In many ways the Legion will always remain a mystery to outsiders. Only a Legionnaire can truly understand its strange blend of apparently archaic tradition and modern military application; its ability to mold men of various races, nationalities, and religions into a crack fighting force, and its paradoxical survival in an era of increased political sensitivity and high-tech weaponry.

Since its inception in 1831, the "old Legion" has fought in all of France's wars and skirmishes. Campaigns in Algeria, the Crimea, Italy, Mexico, France, Tonkin, Dahomey, Madagascar, WWI, Morocco, Syria, WWII, Indochina (where the Legion's strength rose to thirty-five thousand men), Suez, and France's last colonial struggle in Algeria, secured the Legion's place in military history. More recent deployments in Zaire, Chad, Central Africa, Cambodia, Lebanon, Somalia, the Gulf, Rwanda, and Bosnia have confirmed the Legion's reputation as a flexible, ever-ready military asset.

Formerly, Legion recruiting standards varied, depending upon France's military needs. In times of war or costly colonial campaigns, the recruiting officers applied less stringent regulations in accepting foreigners to Legion ranks. The cloak of official anonymity and the ability to change one's name eased the process. Today, although anonymity and name changes are still guaranteed, the Legion is turning away recruits. Approximately ten thousand hopeful foreigners now volunteer annually, but only thirteen hundred are accepted.

Times have changed, and the Legion has changed with them. Today's Legionnaire may be a scuba diver, a specialist in mountain warfare, the driver of an AMX tank, a computer technician, or a free-fall parachutist. Although its headquarters and regiments are now based in France, permanent Foreign Legion garrisons are currently maintained in the Republic of Djibouti, Tahiti, French Guiana, and the Comoro Islands.

No unit sums up the Legion's contemporary role and mission better than the 2nd Parachute Regiment (*2ème Régiment Étranger des Parachutistes*) based at Camp Raffalli, near Calvi, Corsica. The paras of the Legion, described by Bruce Quarrie in his book, *The World's Elite Forces*, as "some of the most skilled and dangerous soldiers on earth," are two-time volunteers—initially for service in the Legion and then for training as parachutists. These *chuters* are truly the "elite of the elite," bolstered by a professional officer corps and a cadre of noncoms of various origins described as "second to none" by foreign military observers. These cadres believe in the old Legion maxim, "Hard Training—Easy War."

The 2nd Parachute Regiment's reputation as one of the world's finest rapid intervention units is based principally on its versatility. As the only parachute unit of the Foreign Legion, it fits easily into its classic wartime role as an integral part of the French Army's 11th Parachute Division. Meanwhile, it plays a spearhead role in smaller, commando assignments protecting French interests in an unsettled world of limited-intensity conflicts and terrorism. It also participates in operations involving international military cooperation such as the Gulf War, Somalia, and Bosnia.

Seven years after my first contact with the Foreign Legion in Marseille, I again encountered the Legion in Indochina. I had been assigned to cover the Franco-Vietminh war as an official war correspondent for the U.S. Information Agency. In this role, I accompanied the Legion on operations in the grey mud of the Tonkin Delta, the jungled mountains of northwest Vietnam, and the furnace-hot rubber plantations near Saigon.

It was during this period that I became familiar with the Legion's parachute battalions, including the *2ème BEP* (*Bataillon Étranger Parachutiste*), the forerunner of today's *2ème REP,* (*Régiment Étranger Parachutiste*). They were unique, battle-hardened units, heavy with German personnel (postwar Legion recruiters did not probe too deeply into a German volunteer's military past) and seeded with diminutive Vietnamese recruits to compensate for continued losses in the never-ending *sale-guerre* that was completely draining the French Army.

Although today's versatile and highly mobile 2nd Foreign Legion Parachute Regiment differs greatly from the heavy, classic airborne battalions of the Indochina conflict, it shares with them a proud history and certain aspects of their "warrior-monk" tradition. Just as important has been the regiment's ability to shed outdated concepts and update procedures to fit new requirements and tactical developments.

My earlier contacts with the Foreign Legion continued during the 1970s while I served as U.S. Consul General in Marseille. Later, as a full-time writer, I visited various Legion units at Orange, Laudun, and Castelnaudary when gathering material for magazine and newspaper articles.

Certain basic research for this book was accomplished at the Archives of the French Army Ground Forces at the Château de Vincennes, the Legion headquarters and Archives at Aubagne, and the Legion's Retirement Home at Puyloubier. However, the time spent with the active-duty officers, noncoms, and men of the 2nd Foreign Legion Parachute Regiment at Camp Raffalli, near Calvi, Corsica, as well as observing the regiment's jump training, firing, and field exercises was the most rewarding.

The 2nd REP appears to have found the practical balance and answer to today's politico-military challenges that require rapid, effective action. This crack unit of thirteen hundred and fifty men and sixty officers is a model of the "lean and mean" formula. Its contemporary operational history has proven that small can, indeed, be beautiful in the military sense.

Acknowledgments

My thanks to Maj. Gen. Christian J. Piquemal, commander of the French Foreign Legion, and a former office of the Legion's 2nd Parachute Regiment, whose enthusiasm and assistance were invaluable in completing this book. My thanks also to Lt. Col. Michel Germain, the Legion's communications officer, for his time and patience, and all the officers and men at Aubagne Headquarters who agreed to be interviewed. I would also like to thank Adjudant-Chef* Kaan and the staff of the Legion's museum and archives at Aubagne; the staff of the French Army Ground Forces Historical Service at the Château de Vincennes; and the staff and residents of the Legion's retirement home at Puyloubier. A special thanks to Dr. Luc Valery, consul general of Senegal in Marseille and an old friend, who used his long-time contacts with the Legion to help me prepare this book project.

The amount of cooperation I received at the 2nd Parachute Regiment's base at Camp Raffalli, Calvi, Corsica, makes it impossible to cite everyone who was of assistance. Special mention, however, must go to Lt. Col. Yannick Blevin, deputy commander of the 2nd REP, who, in the absence in Central Africa of the commander, Col. Bruno Dary, saw that all doors were opened to me; to Maj. Bruno Brottier, the regiment's executive officer who, doubling as communications officer, arranged my scheduling and appointments; and to Lt. Col. Philippe Rideau, the operations officer, who kept me informed of upcoming events and exercises.

My thanks also to Capt. François Plessy who greeted me on my arrival at Calvi airport and insisted that I share his family's Sunday lunch; to Capt. Patrice Valentin who took me into the Corsican maquis to observe his heavy mortar teams at work; to Capt. Brice Houdet of the CEA who provided me with full access to his company; to Capt. Bruno Schiffer of the deep penetration Commando Section and his staff who briefed me thoroughly on their operations and allowed me to observe their free-fall technique; to Capt. Eric des Minieres who explained in detail the 3rd Company's working link with the U.S. Marines in Somalia; to Company *Adjudant* (warrant officer) Zigic, a decorated veteran of Somalia who, in addition to giving me his views on to-

---

*Roughly equal to a U.S. Army chief warrant officer. See Appendix 1 for equivalent ranks.

day's Legion, showed me Calvi by night; to *Adjudant* Etievant, a specialist in jungle warfare, who explained the basic rules for survival in the rain forest; to *Sergent-Chef* (first sergeant) Pastrovicchio, who received me royally in his mess kitchen and confirmed my belief that the Legion still eats well; to *Sergent* (sergeant) Phillips, regimental photographer, who helped me in many ways and— as jumpmaster—insisted I wear a parachute when near the gaping rear door of a Transall; to *Caporal-Chef* B. (senior corporal), a former leatherneck, who gave me a quick course in Legion weaponry; to *Caporal-Chef* Woussen for his hospitality as president of the *Foyer des Caporaux-Chefs;* to the late *Caporal-Chef* Ofria—a fellow Californian—whose insights into the life of a Legion para were both measured and sound; to the aspirants, the young officer candidates; doctors, dentists, pharmacists, and technicians, doing their military service as volunteers in the 2nd REP, who often shared a dinner table and conversation with me at the Caserne Sampiero; and my personal thanks to the staff of the Caserne Sampiero in the historic Citadel of Calvi where I was housed and fed. Finally, my deep appreciation to my daughter Shawn who, despite her busy schedule in Marseille, provided information and translation backup following my departure from France.

A number of books back-stopped my personal research. These include: Geoffrey Bocca, *The Secret Army* (Englewood Cliffs, New Jersey: Prentice Hall Inc. 1968); Jean-Francois Chauvel, *Kolwezi, les Secret Du Raid* (Paris: Olivier Orban, 1978); Pierre Dufour, *2e REP—Action Immediate* (Paris: Charles Lavauzelle, 1994) Roger Faligot, Pascal Kop, *La Piscine, les Services Secret Français 1944–1948* (Paris: Éditions du Seuil, 1985) Paul Gaujac, *Histoire des parachutistes Français* (Vincennes: Bureau de rédaction Littéraire, SHAT, 1991) Pierre Mac-Orlan, *Pages de Gloire de la Légion Étrangere* (Paris: Andre Martel, 1952) Simon Murray, *Legionnaire; My Five Years in the French Foreign Legion* (New York: Times Books, 1978); Douglas Porch, *The French Foreign Legion* (New York: Harper Collins, 1991); Bruce Quarrie, *The World's Elite Forces* (London: Octopus Books, 1985); Revue Historique des Armées, *Légion Étrangère 1831–1981* (Château de Vincennes, 1981); Serge, *Filles du Sud et Képis Blancs* (Paris: Éditions Baudiniere, 1952); Pierre Sergent, *2eme R.E.P.* (Paris: Presses de la Cité, 1984); John Robert Young/Erwan Bergot, *La Légion Étrangère* (Paris: Robert Laffont, 1984).

1

—⟨⟨⟩⟩⟩—

BIRTH OF A LEGEND

Forty years ago a new brotherhood of fighting men was born at the other end of the world: the parachutists of the Legion. From the old Legion, they inherited the traditions of rigour, solidity, discipline, devotion; from the parachutists came youth, flexibility, enthusiasm, and a taste for the unusual. They quickly formed units unique to their kind: The *Bataillons Étrangers de Parachutistes.*

> General Guignon, 1988
> former commander,
> 2nd REP 1980–82

In the late spring there is still snow on Mount Cinto, Corsica's highest mountain, and the other peaks dominating the deep, crescent-shaped Bay of Calvi. A fine sea mist blurs the sweep of the long sand beach and hangs in the branches of the pines. The early morning sun bursts through the scudding clouds, painting the houses of the old city and the walls of the historic Citadel a warm shade of rose. The last trace of the winds of le mistral blows through the narrow, cobblestoned streets within the ancient fortress. A small colony of stray cats emerges from shelter on the leeward side of the ramparts to forage for food. Yacht halyards in the marina beat a faint metallic tattoo against the masts. Calvi's main street, the Boulevard Wilson, is practically deserted, but a few early risers are in the cafés, sipping their espresso and reading the Corsican editions of *Nice Matin* and *Le Provençal.*

An unholy roar echos over the bay from the direction of the airport at Saint Catherine. Shortly thereafter, the first roar is followed by another, then another. The high-powered Rolls Royce engines of the French Air Force C-160 Transalls are at full throttle as they speed and thump along the runway, rise over the bay, and climb toward the heights above Lumio. Later, following the coastline toward Ile Rousse, they bank sharply and begin their return to Calvi, descending lower over the bay on a steady run toward the Drop Zone (DZ-*Zone du Saut*) of Camp Raffalli.

Suddenly, the sky is filled with parachutes, as the men of the 2nd Foreign Legion Parachute Regiment, (2nd REP) spill rapidly out of the transports one after another. The distant, fast-falling dots stabilize under their opening canopies, then swing rapidly to the ground. A senior Legion jumpmaster watches their descent from the edge of the DZ with a critical eye. Nearby, a detachment of recruits with short-cropped hair marches along the paved street of the camp with the traditional slow pace of the Legion. They are singing the regimental song, a deep-throated chant, the vocal pauses punctuated by the rhythmic thumping of boots.

"We are the men of the assault troops," the apprentice paras bellow, "We not only have arms, but the devil marches with us . . ."

Some of the newcomers risk the *caporal-chef's* (senior corporal's) fury as they glance up at the distant parachutes, wondering how they will perform when the time comes for their first jump.

The din of military aircraft, the blossoming of parachutes, and the rattle of automatic weapons firing from distant ranges are everyday occurrences to the people of Calvi and the mountainous region of Balagne, whose ancestors were no strangers to the sounds of warfare and a military presence. The Romans found the Bay of Calvi a perfect stopover for their foraging fleets. Placed under the protection of Genoa in 1278, the city was strongly fortified by the Genoese.

Various nations and states envied both Calvi's strategic position in the Mediterranean and its sheltered harbor. The city was attacked in 1284 by a fleet from Pisa. An army of the king of Aragon seized Calvi in 1420 and held it for a year until its Spanish garrison was annihilated. Papal forces tried to take the city twice without success. In 1553 and 1555 the city repulsed the attacks of a Franco-Turkish fleet with such determination that the Genoese granted a plaque to the city that reads *Civitas Calvi semper fidelis* (City of Calvi always faithful). The plaque remains in place today at the entrance to the Citadel. Calvi also lays claim to being the birthplace of Christopher Columbus, a distinction disputed by Genoa.

Calvi became French in 1768; in 1794, the Corsican patriot Pascal Paoli, whose forces were supported by a British fleet, laid siege to the city. During the siege, which lasted from June 25 to August 5, Calvi received twenty-four thousand cannon balls, forty-five hundred bombs, and fifteen hundred shells. The future Lord Nelson lost his eye during this siege while serving as a Royal Navy captain. British forces occupied Calvi upon the city's surrender and remained there for two years. France regained Calvi in 1797, following Napoleon's victories in Italy.

On May 20, 1815, Napoleon wrote to his Minister of War Marshal Davout,

Prince d'Eckmuhl, about the defense of his island birthplace, particularly the city of Calvi.

"Put some funds at the disposal of the engineers and artillery in Corsica," the emperor ordered, ". . . Corsica has no real defenses. We must concentrate our expenditure on Calvi to put it in order." He concluded his letter by giving detailed tactical instructions. If the enemy landed on the island, his troops should defend the ground "foot-by-foot" before falling back on the Citadel of Calvi to withstand a siege until help arrived.

More recently, during World War II, the Italian Air Force occupied the airstrip at Fiume Secco, immediately outside the city. Calvi was liberated from the Germans by the *Premier Bataillon de Choc* of the Free French forces in September 1943. This unit then trained at Calvi for the landing in southern France on August 15, 1944.

The U.S. Army Air Force flew B-17s from the reconditioned Italian airstrip after the liberation of Corsica. One of these aircraft—ditched on its return from a mission—still lies under thirty meters of water not far from the Citadel.

The *Premier Choc* returned to Calvi in 1956, and two years later occupied the camp of Fiume Secco—future site of Camp Raffalli—using the airstrip for their Junkers 52 aircraft. With the dissolution of the *Premier Choc* in 1963, a detachment of the 2nd REP was installed at Fiume Secco. The entire regiment moved from Bou Sfer, Algeria, to Fiume Secco in 1967. The camp installation was then renamed *Camp Raffalli* after Major Raffalli, a commander of the 2nd Foreign Legion Parachute Battalion, killed in action during the Indochina War.

There are few military installations in the world that can boast such a location. The stuccoed, red tile-roofed buildings of the camp face the blue Mediterranean with their backs to a rugged mountain range. The beach is 500 meters from the sentry-guarded entrance gate. Neatly arranged streets divide company barracks, command center, utility buildings, garages, parachute maintenance hangars, hospital, mess halls, leisure and sport installations, the regimental museum, the cinema and lecture hall. Pines, palms, magnolias, century plants, and eucalyptus grow in the planted park areas.

The *voie sacré* (sacred path) leading to the regiment's monument, dedicated to Legion parachutists killed in action during various campaigns, is just within the entry to the camp. The monument itself with the Latin inscription *More Majorum* (in the footsteps of our predecessors) was brought to Corsica from the 2nd REP's (*Régiment Étranger des Parachutistes*) former base at Sétif, Algeria, after the war in Algeria ended. The wall of the headquarters building, just behind the monument, bears the Legion's motto, *Legio Patria Nostra* (The Legion is our country).

Although the Legion paras may profit personally from the Corsican climate and the beauty of the site, the true value of Camp Raffalli is what it offers in the way of training areas. The regiment's drop zone (DZ) is located on the edge of the camp. Once back on the ground, paras can, if need be, gather their chutes and walk a short distance to their barracks.

The amphibious training center, located on the beach at the mouth of the Figarella River, is across the road from the camp. French Navy submarines slip into the bay to pick up paras from the amphibious center for subaqua infiltration exercises.

A mountain chalet at the 1,300 meter-high Vergio Pass, a ninety-mile truck ride from Calvi, houses Legionnaires involved in mountain warfare training and preparing for qualification as military skiers and alpine climbers. Live-fire ranges with pop-up targets in the mountains closer to Calvi provide realistic weapons training. The village of Fraselli is used for exercises in house-to-house fighting.

The maquis, the wild, rough terrain of Corsica, provides the 2nd REP with a unique and difficult training ground. The rugged, brush-covered hills look beautiful from a distance, but the myrtle, cactus, six-foot-tall heather, spiky gorse, barbary fig, arbutus, and rock rose combine to form uniform-tearing barriers that can dull even the sharpest machete. Legionnaires humping heavy weapons over the steep hills and narrow goat paths of northwest Corsica soon develop hard muscles and a very special physical stamina.

A guidebook explaining Corsica to summer tourists states that "the climate varies from Alpine to Mediterranean." To the paras of Camp Raffalli, this translates as "freezing to hot." It means digging in during exercises on snow-covered, windswept mountain slopes or lying in the dust under a fierce sun, blinking away the sweat to line up the sights of their FAMAS rifles on a distant target. Such extremes serve the Legionnaires well later when they find themselves wintering in the hills of Bosnia or patrolling the Chadian desert.

A low, slate-roofed, stone-walled building near the entry to Camp Raffalli houses the Regimental Museum. A marble slab in front of the entrance bears the inscription, "The Sun Never Sets on Earth Soaked with the Blood of Legionnaires."

This museum is the repository of the 2nd REP's history and traditions. It is a cool, quiet place where newly assigned officers and men begin to understand the unit they have joined and what the future might entail. A stained glass window bearing the regimental insignia casts a multicolored light on the interior entrance hall. Battalion and regimental flags and various athletic trophies for marathons, boxing, and markmanship share space with a citation from Xavier Colonna, Calvi's former mayor, reaffirming the regiment's close relations with the city and its inhabitants. A large, professional watercolor of paras dropping into the Bay of Calvi with the Citadel and city in the distance underscores this relationship.

Two Soviet heavy (AA) machine guns and an AT-3 SAGGER A rocket launcher captured at Faya Largeau, Chad, during operation *Épervier* (Sparrowhawk) in the late 1980s are displayed in the hall. A slow walk from room to room leads from battle to battle and operation to operation.

The regiment's predecessor, the *2e Bataillon Étranger de Parachutistes*, or *2nd BEP*, is represented by a photo taken in 1952 of the battalion in action at Na San in northwest Vietnam; a bronze temple bell from Tonkin, a yellow-starred, red flag of the Vietminh, and a framed photo of a fatally wounded Major Raffalli, the battalion commander, being evacuated for medical treatment in Hanoi. The thin, pallid officer is clutching the battalion's flag to his chest. The same, weatherstained *fanion* now hangs beside the photo. The display on Indochina also includes a barbed pungi trap, captured Vietminh documents, an enemy helmet, a relief map of Dien Bien Phu, and additional captured weapons.

A display of citations and decorations includes the *fourragère* in the colors of the Legion of Honor. The 2d REP is the only unit of the French Army Ground Forces to have received that distinction in Indochina. The regimental flag is decorated with the croix de guerre with six palms. In addition, the 2nd Company's *fanion* is decorated with the croix de guerre with one palm.

Other sections of the museum include captured battle flags and weapons of the Algerian National Liberation Front, the pro-Libyan FROLINAT in Chad, the "Tigers" of Kolwezi, and the PLO in Beirut. A new museum addition houses material relating to the regiment's service in the Gulf War, Somalia, and Bosnia. The former campaign is represented by photos of the regiment's deep penetration commandos operating within Iraqi lines at As Salman. A collection of arms from Sarajevo is dominated by a photo of Legionnaire 1st Class Miroslav Benki, "*Mort pour la France*" on February 11, 1993 at Sarajevo airport. Considering the regiment's ongoing assignments, additional museum extensions undoubtedly will be needed.

Watching the jump training at Camp Raffalli, speculating on the thoughts of the newly arrived recruits, or wandering through the regimental museum, a simple question emerges. When or how did it all begin?

One of the first recorded French references to parachuting was a report from a missionary newly returned from China many years ago. He brought with him a parchment describing an emperor's crowning ceremony in 1306 during which acrobats dropped from tall towers aided by makeshift parachutes. More than three hundred years later, a French ambassador to Siam reported local acrobats performing in the same manner. During the 1700s, balloonists in Europe, concerned with their own safety, began experimenting with crude, framework parachutes that could return them to earth if their balloons exploded or burst into flames.

In 1889 Leroux and Loyal, two American balloonists, blown out to sea, were rescued by a German ship on its way to Europe. The Americans were then invited to visit Germany by the German government to give several parachuting demonstrations that were particularly appreciated by the German Army.

World War I and the advent of air warfare speeded the development of military parachuting. Initially, some of the "knights of the air" considered the parachute beneath their dignity. The development of more effective aerial weaponry and heavy air crew losses soon changed their minds.

During the 1920s, U.S. Gen. Billy Mitchell—in addition to horrifying naval brass by sinking the decommissioned battleship *Ostfriesland* by aerial bombing—promoted the idea of landing troops behind enemy lines by parachute. Despite an impressive demonstration, his superior officers shelved the proposal.

Not all military men were so shortsighted. The Soviet Army dropped twelve fully armed parachutists behind "enemy lines" during an exercise in 1930. By 1934, the regular paratroopers of the Soviet Army were participating by the hundreds in maneuvers. At one operation near Kiev, foreign military attachés watched in amazement as twelve hundred parachutists were dropped, followed by twenty-five hundred others, with their full equipment and supplies.

The French quickly indicated considerable interest concerning this new form of warfare. In 1935, after extensive negotiations, France was permitted to send a military mission to the Soviet Union to study the organization and tactics being developed by the Russians. Capt. Fred Geille, a World War I ace and former infantry officer, led the mission. He returned to France in 1936, after earning Soviet Parachute Instructor's Qualification No. 111. Geille established an instruction center at an airfield near Avignon where sixty recruits were trained to form two *Groupes d'Infantrie de l'Air*, or Airborne Infantry. Two years later, the German High Command formed its first parachute Battalion.

The early phase of World War II was a period of confusion and frustration for the untested French paras. Shifted from North Africa to northern France, their planned actions aborted, they found themselves fighting as ground assault troops in Alsace. They were then sent to Algeria where their possible usefulness ended with the signing of the Franco-German armistice.

On June 18, 1940, General deGaulle broadcast his famous call from London for volunteers to join the Free French forces and continue the fight against the Axis forces. In August, he ordered the establishment of a French parachute unit. These *Parachutistes des Forces Françaises Libres* were integrated into the British Special Air Services (SAS) under the legendary Col. David Stirling. Specializing in clandestine operations and lightning raids, the French paras distinguished themselves in France, Syria, Crete, Tripoli, and Tunisia. Reconstituted into the 2nd and 3rd *Régiments de Chasseurs Parachutistes,* some of these shock troops were dropped into Normandy before D-Day and assisted in the liberation of Brittany. As part of the 1st Allied Airborne Division, they later fought in the Ardennes and Holland and participated in the final defeat of Nazi Germany.

It was the coming struggle for Indochina, however, that would occasion the rapid development of new French parachute units and their deployment in a different and difficult form of warfare.

France had hardly caught its breath from both the occupation and the liberation before its troops were involved in a distant conflict. Attempts to negotiate peacefully the fate of French Indochina between a French government, determined to reestablish its presence there, and Ho Chi Minh's Communist and nationalist Vietminh, equally determined to achieve independence, failed in 1946. A French Expeditionary Force of thirty-five thousand men under the command of Gen. Jacques Philippe LeClerc, whose armored division had liberated Paris, was now attempting to "pacify" Indochina. But the pacification of a postwar revolutionary Vietnam was proving much more difficult than the early colonial expeditions when order could be restored with a few companies of native troops and an iron hand.

Quickly recognizing the probable cost of a new war in Southeast Asia, General LeClerc had urged the French government to negotiate with the Vietminh. More politicized generals, civilian officials, and the colonial lobby in Paris had supported the use of force—and won.

A year of inconclusive, costly fighting had proven that the tactics used in the European campaigns had little application in the paddies and jungles of Vietnam. Many shortsighted military traditionalists ignored this truth. But there were other officers who recognized that classic road-bound units, heavy with armor, were ineffective in fast-moving anti-guerrilla operations.

If Algeria and Sidi-bel-Abbès were the Legion's home and base, Indochina had been its second residence. The Legion had played a leading role in France's annexation and conquest of Indochina. In 1883 the Legion was sent to help enforce France's role as a protectorate power in Tonkin. This put the Legionnaires, Marines, and colonial troops on a collision course with the Black Flag pirates, a well-armed, semiofficial Chinese force far superior in number to the French Expeditionary Corps. The Legion participated in the capture of Black Flag citadels at Sontay and Bac-Ninh. The defense of Tuyen-Quang, a town northwest of Hanoi on the Clear River, became a part of Legion history. Three hundred and ninety Legionnaires, some Tonkinese riflemen, artillerymen, and a few engineers held off a besieging force of twenty thousand determined Black Flags from November 23, 1884, until March 3, 1885.

The Legionnaires who fought and died defending the bamboo-reinforced walls at Tuyen-Quang were tough, sun-bronzed men with few illusions. They had been sent on their way by General de Negrier with a brutally frank message. "You, Legionnaires, you are soldiers in order to die and I'm sending you where one does."

The eventual domination of Vietnam, Cambodia, and Laos and their integration into the French colonial empire ushered in a period of relative peace in Indochina. The Legion and units of *La Coloniale* found themselves in garrisons maintaining order and a French presence. The Legionnaires followed their tradition as builders of roads, bridges, and barracks. The occasional flurry of smuggling, piracy, or anti-French rebellion kept the Legion from losing its fighting edge. For many Legionnaires, colonial service in Indochina was more appealing than close order drill at Sidi-bel-Abbès or slogging through the Sahara in search of elusive, rebellious tribesmen.

No small part of this appreciation had to do with the slow pace of everyday life, the beauty of the countryside, and—above all—the attractiveness of the local women. Although the Legion did not integrate locally as extensively as the troops of the colonial infantry, they, too, fell under the spell of this strange and exotic land. Few Legionnaires, particularly the veteran noncoms, were without their *congaï,* a substitute wife who shared their bed, prepared their meals, and kept their uniforms cleaned and pressed. For *les anciens d'Indo,* Cambodia was enjoyable, Vietnam was pleasurable, and Laos was heaven on earth owing to its isolation and particularly compliant women. Some young, first assignment officers were shocked by what they found in Indochina and attempted to whip their small detachments into regulation Legion shape. Most of them, however, soon surrendered to the ritual of the afternoon *sieste,* the sundown pastis, and the soothing presence of a graceful Cambodian, Laotian, or Vietnamese mistress.

During the late 1940s and early 1950s, the successors to the Legionnaires who endured the siege of Tuyen-Quang were battling over the same territory with another implacable enemy—the Communist Vietminh under the leadership of Ho Chi Minh and the redoubtable Gen. Vo Nguyen Giap. Legion infantry battalions and armored vehicles of the 1st Legion Cavalry Regiment were clashing with the Vietminh in Tonkin, Annam, and Cochin China. Legionnaires were participating in large-scale operations as members of a *Groupe Mobile* (Regimental Combat Team), participating in ambushes and patrols of company and platoon strength, and garrisoning fortified strong points designed to protect strategic regions and communications routes.

But General Giap's troops flowed undetected from their camouflaged mountain hideouts into the crucial Tonkin Delta, the coastal plains of Central Vietnam and the reed-filled swamps of the Mekong Delta to cut roads, ambush convoys, and mount nocturnal attacks on unsuspecting French outposts. In most operational zones, the night belonged to the Vietminh, the roads were closed, and the French were buttoned down until dawn within their fortifications. By the time a *Groupe Mobile* was alerted to relieve a besieged post and arrived on the scene, it often found a smoking ruin with its garrison lying dead among the shattered defenses.

When the Vietminh began fielding regular units of regimental and divisional strength, the French recognized the war had entered a new phase. The enemy was now showing a willingness to confront larger French units. Even more disturbing was their ability to stand and fight over a more extended period.

It had become obvious by 1948 that the French High Command required more flexibility in dealing with the Vietminh threat. In practical terms, this meant the establishment of a dependable rapid reaction, airborne force in Indochina. The new parachute battalions were built on the model of the wartime *Chasseurs Parachutistes* of the regular French Army or formed as units wearing the anchor of the colonial infantry. The large, traditional Foreign Legion presence in Indochina made the establishment of Legion parachute units a practical proposition.

On July 1, 1948, the *1er Bataillon Étranger de Parachutistes* (1st Foreign Legion Parachute Battalion) was established at Khamisis, Algeria. On July 19, 1948, a secret order from the French Secretary of State for the Armed Forces, signed by the chief of staff of the armed forces, General Revers, was addressed to the senior general commanding all French troops in Morocco and the colonel commanding the Foreign Legion base at Sidi-bel-Abbès, Algeria: "I have the honor to inform you that I have decided to create, as of August 1, 1948, the 2nd Foreign Legion Parachute Battalion (2nd BEP). This unit, intended for the Far East, will be of the type defined in (order No.) 4.77 EMA/1.0.S. of May 24, 1948, for the 1st Foreign Legion Parachute Battalion. . ."

In addition to the practicalities of dealing with personnel, equipment, and training, the necessity for speed in the order's execution was underlined in Section V of the document: "The 2nd BEP should be ready for embarkation beginning December 1, 1948." The formation of a 3rd (depot) Battalion was planned for April 1949.

The assembly, organization, equipping, and training of a viable parachute battalion in four months borders on the miraculous. It also displays an element of what an indulgent commentator might call élan and a more critical observer describe as recklessness.

Certain problems had already arisen with the 1st BEP. The high command had ordered this battalion to depart for the Far East on October 24, 1948.

But the Inspector General of the Foreign Legion, with the approval of the commanding general of the 25th Airborne Division and the colonel commanding the regimental depot, had warned in a secret document of "grave consequences," if the airborne battalions were deployed too rapidly:

> Installed June 15 in bivouac 10 kilometers from Philippeville (Algeria), the 1st BEP was not able to begin its training until July 1st.
>
> The arrival of its full complement of cadre, its reinforcement elements, the late reception of its materiel (clothing, armament, ammunition, radios, etc.), was spread between July 20th and September 20th, and the difficulties of adaptation to the French language by its men, have considerably delayed and impeded the military training, technical instruction and cohesion of its units. But the most serious inconvenience of the immediate use of the 1st BEP in the Far East stems from:
>
> –its deficiency in non-commissioned officer cadre (50 percent)
>
> –The incomplete training of its various specialists (machine gunners, mortar crews, radiomen, repairmen, and medics).
>
> In sum, the 1st BEP is actually undergoing a breaking-in period, but the short time left before its embarkation won't allow it to fill the inevitable gaps of a too hasty training.

Despite this well-reasoned argument, the pressure was on, and the decision had been made. The 1st BEP was destined to come ashore at Haiphong in November 1948 and was plunged directly into combat operations. The 2nd BEP underwent the same hurried preparation and arrived at Saigon on February 9, 1949. The battalion was rushed to action in Cambodia and later in Central Vietnam where it won its first croix de guerre.

Within months of their arrival, the Legion paras had joined the other parachute battalions of the French Expeditionary Corps as the reserve force "firemen" of the Indochina war. They were constantly on call to relieve posts or units under heavy attack, to spearhead large-scale operations, and to drop into enemy territory on surprise raids. Control and liaison for such operations were particularly difficult in the rugged jungle terrain. During the American war in Vietnam, chopper-borne airmobile operations largely replaced the parachute drops of the earlier Indochina war.

The French defeat at Dong-Khe on September 18, 1950, and the subsequent evacuation of the important post of Cao-Bang, found the Legionnaires of the 1st BEP jumping in as reinforcements. This major military disaster had the Vietminh rolling up the French posts along the Vietnam-Chinese border one after another. It was also marked by grave command errors and hesitations that cost thousands of lives and left the Vietminh with huge quantities of French supplies, including two thousand tons of munitions and four thousand submachine guns.

The 1st BEP arrived on the scene as retreating French columns were fighting through large, well-set Vietminh ambushes. After a deadly firefight at Na-Keo, the battalion's strength was down to 400 men, and its flexibility was limited by the wounded it was transporting by makeshift litter over tortuous terrain. More violent fighting in the jagged limestone hills and jungle valleys was marked by the successive deaths of all the company commanders and the battalion commander, Major Segretain. Only one officer, Captain Jean-pierre, and twenty-eight men survived the butchery. By October 7, 1950, the 1st BEP had ceased to exist as a unit.

In Paris, Rene Pleven the *president du conseil* reported details of the disaster to the grim-faced members of the French Chamber of Deputies.

"The two battalions of the Foreign Legion (1st BEP and 3rd Bn. of the 3rd Infantry Regiment) have suffered the heaviest losses," Pleven explained. "True to the tradition of their Corps, they sacrificed themselves to protect the withdrawal of other units."

For the next three years, the 2nd BEP and the reconstituted 1st BEP were in continual combat throughout Vietnam. In March 1951, the dynamic Gen. Jean de Lattre de Tassigny, commander of the French Expeditionary Force, had approved the reactivation of the 1st BEP and insisted that a company of Indochinese paras be added to its complement. This move supported de Lattre's desire to see the "loyal" Vietnamese participate more directly in combat. It also encouraged the Legion parachute battalions to open their ranks to more local recruits. This enabled them to fill gaps caused by battle casualties more rapidly than by waiting for replacements from Algeria.

On September 11, 1952, General Gonzalez de Linares, the Ground Force Commander, North Vietnam, signed a grim open letter to the officers and men of the 2nd BEP:

"Major Raffalli," the general wrote, "died during the night of September 10–11, 1952, in the Saigon Hospital. . . . After having created, trained, animated with his ardour, and led the 2nd BEP in combat, he fell, gravely wounded, on September 1 at Chuyen-My-Troung-Ha during the last action he led with you." Reviewing the constant engagement of the 2ème BEP "in the Delta, the Mountainous and Central Regions" the general spoke of the "brilliant personality" of this "prestigious leader" and closed by mentioning the "magnificent tradition Major Raffalli has left with the 2nd BEP."

A wiry *Niçois* and graduate of Saint Cyr, Barthélèmy Raffalli had first served with the Algerian Spahis (cavalry) for eight years until 1943. Then, with Free French forces fighting on the side of the Allies, he campaigned in Italy where he was detached to the infantry. There he was badly wounded leading a company of Moroccan riflemen and was made a *chevalier* of the Legion of Honor. Volunteering for parachute training after the war, he served in Indochina with the 1st BEP before taking command of the 2nd BEP in November 1950.

Noted for his bravery, he led his battalion through the heavy fighting at Nghia-Lo, Colonial Route 6, at Bavi, and in the Tonkin Delta. His conduct of these actions earned him the title of *officier* of the Legion of Honor.

Shortly after turning over command of the 2nd REP in late August 1952, a regrettable decision ended Major Raffalli's career. He agreed to command the 2nd REP on one last operation. It was a fatal gesture. While he was leading from the front, a Vietminh sharpshooter found his mark, dropping the major into the Delta mud.

Posthumously named a *commandeur* of the Legion of Honor, Raffalli had brought a unique verve to his command of the 2nd BEP—the same military panache that is nurtured and preserved today in the camp that bears his name.

If the Indochina War produced more than its share of heroes, it was also a hell for the combat troops involved. The implacable heat of the Mekong Delta, the bone-chilling *crachin* rains of Tonkin, and the steamy miasma of the jungles combined with tropical diseases to create recurrent gaps in the Legion's ranks. Owing to limited evacuation facilities, combat casualties often proved fatal. This was particularly true of parachute units dropped far from road links and support units.

Large engagements with clear-cut results were rare. Excerpts from the 2nd BEP's *Journal de Marche* of April 1, 1950 give the tenor of the day-to-day grind when the battalion was operating as a ground force ready reserve:

> Advancing toward the post of Gau Cong in liaison with 'CRABS' (small, American-supplied amphibious vehicles). Observation aircraft signals violent contact 4 kilometers to the south. The Company linked up with the (French) unit attacked and assaulted a large group of rebels at Gio-Non-Nem. Results: Legionnaire Orlowiez dead. Seven wounded: Lt. Delteile; Sgt. Chef Lemoin; Cpl. Menkhaus; Legionnaires Shwarz, Schlack, Hertel, l'Host-Clos. Rebels: 47 dead, 4 prisoners; recuperated, 1 automatic rifle, 1 Hotchkiss machine gun, 1 60mm mortar, 1 50mm mortar, 6 rifles, ammunition, documents. Wounded evacuated to Tra-Vinh.

Although the Legion paras preferred to fight as airborne troops, not all their combat drops were successful. The battalions *Journal de Marche* of November 8, 1952, describes one such operation.

> Battalion receives order to join two other para Bns. in operation "Marion" to establish bridgehead on crossroads of RC-2 and RP-11 near Phu Doan (right bank of the Song Chay) in continuation of Operation "Lorraine." Bn. leaves *Cité Universitaire,* Hanoi, for Gia Lam (airfield) and arrives at 07:20. Loading at

11:20. First jumps at 13:20. Regrouping takes half an hour. Some accidents, some missing.

In no way did the DZ correspond to what had been predicted: we encountered marshy terrain, very high aquatic vegetation, the recuperation of parachutes very difficult. The 6th Company had two dead by '*coup anormal d'artillerie*' (friendly fire).

Caporal-Chef Raymond Sabatier, now living in retirement at the Legion's veteran's home at Puyloubier near Aix-en-Provence, recalls his fighting days in Indochina.

We didn't have much training but we learned very quickly. It was often hand-to-hand and face-to-face. The Viet were indoctrinated and brainwashed. They came on, directly into our fire, carrying bamboo bangalores and woven mats to throw over our barbed wire.

Their political officers had the "*pistolet facile*," (were trigger happy) when it came to punishing their men. They also had special assassination teams to hunt Vietnamese officials and senior officers. We just tried to drop as many of them as possible during a fight and to hit them hard with counterattacks. It was okay during a fight, you didn't have time to think. The worst of it was going through the effects of our dead comrades after a battle. We were a team then, both officers and men, with little difference between us. We had no problems of nationality. Our commanders were true *seigneurs*.

A listing of newly decorated Legionnaires during this period testified to the continued predominance of Germans in the ranks and the increased recruiting of Vietnamese by the Legion.

Croix de Guerre with Bronze Star.

To:	Albuschat, Lothar	Kaiser, Wolfgang
	Birkenbauer, Wilhelm	Marrari, Jean
	Bui Van Xuan	Nguyen Van Mong
	Gonzerowki, Horst	Pham Van Binh

In the winter of 1952, the 2nd BEP joined the garrison at Na-San, a French strongpoint supplied by air in the mountains of northwest Vietnam. This "hedgehog" installation, modeled on British Gen. Orde Wingate's bases behind Japanese lines during the Burma campaign of World War II, was meant to be a center of offensive action. Unfortunately, the position drew Vietminh regular units like flies to honey, and the French were forced to concentrate on their defenses. Nevertheless, the 2nd BEP engaged the enemy well outside the defense perimeter at Co Noi in what proved to be a costly engagement for both sides. No one knew it at the time, but Na-San was a dress rehearsal for the fateful battle of Dien Bien Phu in 1954.

I recall standing on a dirt road just outside Na-San's defense perimeter as the 2nd BEP returned from a battalion size reconnaissance into the surrounding hills. The dusty, perspiring paras came into sight, the brass cartridges in the machine gun belts slung over their shoulders catching the late afternoon sun. Some troopers were smoking cigarettes, others were poking into ration cans with their trench knives, but most had been singing. The deep cadence of a German marching song had seemed strangely out of place among the tall hardwood trees. The officers had quickly silenced their men when they spotted the colonel commanding the strongpoint and the visiting American. As the 2nd BEP slogged past I tried to take a quick census of nationalities: flaxen-haired Germans, stolid Slavs, a scattering of Italians, Spaniards, Hungarians, and numerous Vietnamese. The Vietnamese seemed submerged by their equipment and helmets, periodically breaking into a trot to keep up with their longer-legged comrades. Strangely enough, the impression was not so much of variety but of cohesion as a fighting unit. That night, bundled up in a damp dugout while nervous gunners loosed strings of tracers into the darkness, I slept better knowing the 2nd BEP was on hand.

By the spring of 1953 the 2nd BEP had, indeed, become a stanchion of the French Expeditionary Corps—a unit to be depended on in all circumstances. During this period, the commander of the Sector of Phuc Yen, Tonkin—Lt. Colonel Barral—reported this assessment of the 2nd BEP to the general commanding the Western Zone.

"Supple and maneuverable unit," Barrel wrote, "trained for night action, most disciplined, committing no excesses vis-à-vis the population—which is indispensable in actions carried out within the sector—the 2nd BEP had obtained remarkable results . . ."

The war ground on and during the period April 9–10, 1954, the 2nd BEP, under the command of Maj. Hubert Leisenfelt, was dropped into the shell-scarred, tracer-laced holocaust of Dien Bien Phu. This besieged French strongpoint in the mountains of the T'ai country of northwest Vietnam had been garrisoned by some of the best units of the Expeditionary Corps with the hope of provoking a showdown battle with the Vietminh. French planners had counted on their air force and artillery to annihilate Giap's regulars as they threw themselves at the defensive wire of Dien Bien Phu.

Instead, and against all odds, the Vietminh had moved an overpowering artillery capability to the high ground surrounding the Nam Yum valley, knocked out the vital airstrip and inflicted heavy losses on the defenders. Now, under sustained attack by Giap's divisions since early March, the French were near defeat and the battle to decide the fate of Indochina was drawing to a close.

The 2nd BEP's sister battalion, the 1st BEP, had been in the thick of the fighting at Dien Bien Phu, spearheading many costly counterattacks. The battalion was exhausted and down to less than half its strength. The arrival of the 2nd BEP may have momentarily raised vain hopes, but some realistic combatants saw that fateful airdrop as an empty gesture—too little, too late, and a waste of one of the best parachute units in Indochina.

Lieutenant Rene de Biré (later a general) described the airdrops in a few words. "9th of April 1954, the Company jumped at night. The 1st and 2nd Platoons, equipped during the afternoon, arrived at the airfield at 1800 hrs. They were dropped on (strongpoint) *Claudine* at 0100 hrs. Unforgettable sight: the DC-3 passing through the trajectories of the anti-aircraft fire, the area serving as the DZ pounded by enemy mortar and artillery fire—unreal and terrible—the parachute of *Sergent-Chef* Patri caught fire and the leader of the 1st Platoon, hitting the ground with his chute torched, was gravely wounded. *Sergent* Scoka took command. Captain Delafond had been killed the day before as he touched the ground at the same location. The other drops occurred the following night and it took 48 hours to regroup under constant fire from the *Viets*."

On April 23, 1954, the 2nd BEP was ordered to counterattack toward the secondary strongpoint *Huguette*, recently taken by the Vietminh. The battalion's advance over open ground, a zone that has been described by Legion veterans as "a machine gunner's dream," inflicted heavy casualties. An error—the commander's radio tuned to the wrong frequency—compounded the cost of the action.

In his book, *Ces Hommes de la Legion—qui meurent pour la gloire* (Those Men of the Legion—Who Die for Glory), Lieutenant Ysquierdo of the 2nd BEP told of his own experiences that day. ". . . All that we knew was that we'd have to run a hundred meters across the airstrip to attack the *Viets* who were waiting for us, oust them, kill them, and, in the confusion, organize the terrain and dig in immediately . . . in brief—the routine . . ."

After a French artillery barrage at 1400 the Legionnaires "Left our trenches and ran across the open airstrip swept by bursts of *Viet* machineguns that mowed down the attackers." One Platoon leader, who had lost most of his men in the assault, found himself and his orderly alone in a Vietminh trench, nose-to-nose with the enemy. They managed to escape and rejoined the remnants of the attacking force, "the dead, the wounded, a few untouched men, and the commander of the assault company—a Lieutenant—with a radio."

"Our retreat," Ysquierdo explained, "cost us as much as our attack. In addition to the enemy fire, Legionnaires were blowing up on our own mines. . . . It was a beautiful day, very warm, for those who lived through it."

The 2nd BEP had lost 154 dead and many more wounded. On April 24, the skeletal remains of the 2nd BEP and the 1st BEP were amalgamated into a *Bataillon de Marche Étranger de Parachutistes*. The 160 Legionnaires in this unit fought on until the fortress fell on May 7, 1954.

Thousands of the captured Dien Bien Phu garrison were to die in captivity, struck down by festering wounds, malnutrition, beriberi, dysentery, malaria, and other tropical diseases. The survivors of the parachute battalions, released in the autumn of 1954 under the terms of the Geneva Conference, were gaunt, unsmiling men. Many of them were determined never again to suffer the indignity of defeat or the shame of leaving behind the native troops who had been their comrades-in-arms and remained loyal to France.

Some officers had used their time in the Vietminh prison camps to reflect on the battle and its results. They had also been able to observe the strengths and weaknesses of their revolutionary enemy. Having passed through the Communist "reeducation" process, the former prisoners had developed a fascination for the use of psychological warfare as a tool in politico-military struggles.

By December 1, 1954, the battalion, reconstituted with replacements, had left North Vietnam for Tan Son Nhut airport in Saigon. Installed at Hanh Thong Tay, the paras of the 2nd BEP went to work preparing and managing refugee camps for the hundreds of thousands of non-Communist, mainly Catholic, Vietnamese fleeing North Vietnam. The Legionnaires were later assigned more onerous duties on the Saigon waterfront. There, they replaced Vietnamese dockers during the Tet holiday period and filled the same role when labor unrest and strikes threatened to disrupt normal commerce.

The use of a proud combat unit for such menial tasks did little to maintain the battalion's morale. In early 1955, a report described the battalion's attitude as "sadly skeptical." The report states that most Legion paras considered the United States a "false ally" for not coming to their aid at Dien Bien Phu after the French government requested air support and mentions their "distrust" of both the Vietnamese and the Americans.

The 2nd BEP's Indochina experience was coming to an end. Like other French units, they would leave Vietnam with little fanfare. On November 1, 1955, the Legionnaires hefted their duffle bags and boarded the SS Pasteur lying off Cap Saint-Jacques (Vung Tau) for a seventeen-day voyage to Oran where a new war was waiting for them.

The war for Algerian independence, or the Algerian revolt, depending on your political orientation, had begun in 1954 while the 2nd BEP had been fully occupied in Indochina. What had begun as terrorist bombings and raids on isolated French farms by armed groups of the Algerian FLN (National Liberation Front), had turned into a bloody, no-quarter guerrilla war. Organized FLN units, led in some cases by Algerians who had served with the French Army in Indochina, were ambushing French Army patrols and turning some regions into no-go areas.

This new conflict looked all too familiar to the officers and men of the 2nd BEP. But this time, armed with their own bitter experiences of revolutionary warfare, the paras were determined to be the victors. Was not Algeria, after all, an integral part of France and not a colony? Perhaps more important to the green-bereted paras was the fact that Sidi-bel-Abbès, the cradle of the Legion and its base depot, was located in Algeria. There was, therefore, no question of ceding their home territory to the *fellagha, fell,* or *fellouze,* as the French Army called the activists of the nationalist FLN and the newly consti-tuted ALN, the Army of National Liberation.

2

~~~~~

No Strangers to Death

Jumping is not normal. If it were, we'd have wings.

Senior Jumpmaster,
2nd REP, Calvi, 1995

New recruits joining the Foreign Legion today learn of the Algerian War as part of their overview of the Legion's past. From the moment they enlist, until the moment they are assigned to a regiment, however, they do not have sufficient time for an in-depth history lesson.

The Legion operates numerous recruiting offices in some of France's leading regional cities. Army installations and posts of the national *Gendarmerie* are also authorized to accept foreign applicants and to expedite their travel to the nearest Legion office. These potential Legionnaires must be at least seventeen years of age but not over forty, physically fit, willing to commit themselves for five years, and able to produce some form of identity. The citizens of France are supposedly forbidden from enlisting in the Legion. Some do, however, claiming Belgian, Swiss, or Monagasque citizenship to explain their facility in the French language. Such a minor subterfuge often goes unchallenged by a tolerant recruiter.

With abundant applicants and only thirteen hundred accepted for service, the Legion can now pick and choose. The flow of racial groups and nationalities into the Legion often reflects the influx of individuals fleeing political unrest and economic hardship: White Russians during the Bolshevik Revolution; Spanish Republicans during the rise of Franco; Germans following World War II; central Europeans following Soviet actions in Hungary, Czechoslovakia, and Poland. A number of Cambodians, Laotians, and Vietnamese donned the *képi blanc* in recent decades after fleeing their countries. More recently, a few Bosnians, Serbs, and Croats have made their way to recruiting centers.

High national unemployment can be another spur to enlistment, and media attention may increase interest in the Legion. The Falkland's campaign and its glorification of British arms produced a flow of action-seeking British recruits. A special program on the Legion, screened by a Japanese television network, resulted in the arrival of some Japanese applicants. There are few Americans in the Legion today. Most American Legionnaires have had previous military experience, many in the U.S. Marines or the Army Special Forces. Their regiment of choice is usually the 2nd REP.

The latest official breakdown of the Legion by language group shows: French—47 percent; Slav—20 percent; Spanish/Portuguese—11 percent; English—6 percent; German—5 percent; African—5 percent; Asian—5 percent; Scandinavian—1 percent.

Those recruits planning to opt for the 2nd REP will not see the welcoming gates of Camp Raffalli for some time. They must first travel to the 1st Regiment at Foreign Legion Headquarters in Aubagne, not far from Marseille, for a three-week selection process. This procedure involves I.Q. tests, physical examinations, psychological testing, and security checks. The urgent demand for replacements that led to easy entry into the Legion's ranks—with an attendant lowering of quality—is now a thing of the past.

The Legion's office of security maintains links with INTERPOL and other law enforcement organizations to ensure the barring of any recruits whose names are on police "wanted lists" in Europe and beyond. This is particularly true for those accused of "blood crimes." Nevertheless, the Legion will still provide anonymity and a new name to those with problems in their past, such as domestic difficulties, political persecution, and minor offenses. Journalists seeking photo coverage of Legion units must obtain the permission of those individual Legionnaires in the frame before clicking the shutter.

The reception process at Aubagne manages to shake loose a number of undesirable candidates: naive glory-seekers, psychological misfits, homesick youths, alcoholics, narcotics users, and obvious troublemakers. The current debate on the acceptance of homosexuals in some armed forces has not touched the Legion. Suffice it to say that the environment would not be welcoming. Those recruits who pass the first selection at Aubagne soon learn that the Legion—despite its spit-and-polish on parade—is a fighting outfit, and its members are not strangers to death. This is brought home to the newcomers as they file by the articulated wooden hand of Capt. Jean Danjou in the Legion's Chapel of Remembrance.

This relic commemorates the Battle of Camerone Hacienda (*El Camaron*) in Mexico on April 30, 1863. Captain Danjou commanded a detachment of sixty Legionnaires who fought off two thousand Mexican regulars under a blazing sun during an entire day. The captain was eventually killed, and the five survivors, Mexican bayonets to their chests, were forced to surrender. This was not accomplished, however, until the Legion corporal in charge demanded and received permission for his men to retain their arms and extracted a promise of medical attention for their wounded lieutenant. Danjou's wooden hand, the result of an earlier wound in the Crimea, was recovered and returned to the Legion.

Camerone thus became a symbol of the Legion's fighting spirit and is celebrated yearly on the date of the battle by Legion units around the world. At the Legion's Headquarters at Aubagne, the captain's hand makes its appearance during a ceremony before the *Monument aux Morts,* carried in a special glass-covered case by a Legionnaire—often a senior noncom—chosen by the Legion's commander.

The message of Camerone is not lost on the new recruits. But, if the significance of this ceremony is not fully appreciated, more experienced Legionnaires make sure the newcomers get the message over the traditional *boudin noir* (blood sausage) and *vin rouge* served after the parade. The message of Camerone, simply put, is that a fight to the end against overwhelming odds remains a part of the Legion's tradition. The need to *"faire Camerone"* in modern battle conditions may no longer be either practical or possible. But this philosophy, like the mention of death in many Legion songs, eliminates any illusions that a Legion recruit might have about his chosen calling. He may well complete a course learning how to operate a computer and complex engineering equipment or become expert as a mechanic, but he knows that his basic job is soldiering. He also knows that soldiering means combat, and that any combat could very well result in his death.

The candidate will also learn the seven points of the "Legionnaire's Code of Honor." These commandments are printed on a small pocket card for his ready reference. They state:

1. Legionnaire: you are a volunteer serving France faithfully and with honor.
2. Every Legionnaire is your brother-in-arms, regardless of his nationality, race or creed. You will always demonstrate this by an unwavering and straightforward solidarity that unites members of the same family.
3. Respectful of the Legion's traditions; honoring your superiors; discipline and camaraderie are your strengths; courage and loyalty your virtues.
4. Proud of your status as a Legionnaire, you will display this pride, by your impeccable appearance, your behaviour, ever worthy, though modest, your living quarters, always neat.
5. An elite soldier: you will train vigorously; you will maintain your weapon as if it were your most precious possession; you will keep your body in the peak of condition.
6. A mission given to you becomes sacred; you will accomplish it to its conclusion and at all costs.

   7. In combat: you will act without passion or hatred; you will respect the van-
      quished enemy; never abandon your wounded or dead or under any circum-
      stances surrender your arms.

Once accepted at Aubagne, the recruit—still on sufferance—moves to the
4th (training) Regiment at Castelnaudary in the Department of the Aude.
Here, sixteen weeks of tough basic training is designed to turn him into a
combat soldier. Only after some weeks is a decision made concerning the recruit's future. The majority become Legionnaires and each ceremonially dons
his *képi blanc*. Numerous others will have fallen by the wayside and been rejected. A few, unable to adjust to the life and discipline, may have chosen to
go "over the fence" as deserters. Among these few one often finds disillusioned
romantics who had expected to find military romanticism or a Beau Geste experience.

   An officer described one classic instance of a recruit who had joined the
Legion after his girl had left him for another man. Two months into his new
life as a Legionnaire, he had received a long letter from the girl admitting her
mistake, declaring that he was her true and lasting love, and urging him to
return to her as quickly as possible. The officer, in relating the story, had given
a Gallic shrug of his shoulders, admitting it was difficult—and perhaps impractical—to retain such a frustrated man under those circumstances.

   The task of the training cadre is unique. Each draft of newcomers is a mix
of races, nationalities, religions, and languages. The cadre must mold this heterogeneous, undisciplined mass into a coherent whole, while making sure that
their new charges learn enough French to understand and speak—however
haltingly—the language of command. Throughout the training period, the
cadre will monitor the recruit's performance. They will be alert to both his
strengths and weaknesses. The emergence of leadership qualities may open
the way to special training as a noncom or officer, and the progress of those
with prior military experience will be noted. Ten percent of the Legion's
officers are of foreign origin, and some of these have come from the ranks.
French officers can spend only part of their career in the Legion. Officers and
noncoms of foreign origin can remain in the Legion throughout their careers.
Retirement is compulsory after twenty-five years of service.

   The Legionnaire begins to understand the meaning of the "Legion family"
at Castelnaudary. He learns that the cohesion of the Legion is a large part of
its strength and that mutual support is built into the system. Outsiders may
find it patronizing or surprisingly dated when a Legion officer refers to "my
Legionnaires" and that Legionnaires brace and salute before addressing an
officer. Then, on closer inspection, one finds that the interrelationship between officers, noncoms, and men is close and surprisingly relaxed.

   Despite this togetherness, Legion discipline is strict and applied with impersonal force by the cadre. The Legion's infamous disciplinary companies in North Africa that administered severe punishment to offending Legionnaires have long ceased to exist, but few Legionnaires today willingly buck the system. At the same time, it is the rare Legionnaire who has not spent some time in lockup for minor infractions during his career. A German *caporal-chef* with a few forehead scars, no stranger to barroom brawls, put it succinctly, "With the Legion you know where you stand. If you deserve punishment, you get it. And you're ready for it."

An English-speaking noncom had a message for would-be recruits. "Don't get me wrong," he said, "I volunteered, and I have nothing against the Legion, but anyone thinking of joining should know the facts. They will find it difficult adjusting to Legion life in a strange country, a different culture, and with no knowledge of the language. It isn't playtime . . . they control your life. That said, there is no bigger thrill than marching down the Champs Elysées on Bastille Day with the Legion to the cheers of an admiring crowd."

The training cycle at Castelnaudary ends with four or five days of field exercise or *raid* involving a march of seventy-five miles or more with heavy packs over rough country in freezing winter weather or hot summer conditions. This last test includes river and gorge crossings, night movements, and live-fire combat exercises.

The qualified Legionnaire then receives his regimental assignment. He may return to Aubagne as a member of the 1st Legion Regiment, join the 2nd Legion Infantry Regiment at Nimes, the 1st Legion Cavalry Regiment at Orange, or the 6th Legion Combat Engineer Regiment near Avignon. Some Legionnaires will join overseas units: the 3rd Infantry Regiment at Kourou in French Guiana; the 5th Regiment at Mururoa (the French Nuclear Testing Center) and Tahiti; the 13th demibrigade stationed in the Republic of Djibouti; and the Legion's detachment at Mayotte in the Comoro Islands. Rotating assignments of various regiments may find him in the Central African Republic, Chad, or other African nations linked to France by postcolonial defense agreements. Recent assignments have found the Legion in Lebanon, Somalia, Gabon, Rwanda, and Bosnia. More recently, the armored vehicles of the 1st REC (*Régiment Étranger de Cavalrie*) that faced the Bosnian Serbs on Mount Igman, protecting the supply route into Sarajevo, became part of IFOR, the International Implementation Force.

A limited number of newly formed Legionnaires will head for Calvi and Camp Raffalli. Designated as members of the 2nd REP, they will already have a spring in their step, but it will be some time before they wear the silver wings of a jumper.

The Regimental Drop Zone is comparatively flat and cleared of scrub brush. A scented breeze from the maquis-covered hills riffles the ground cover. At the edge of the camp, a tall observation tower, equipped with wind indicators and radio facilities, dominates the DZ. The tower is manned by one or two observers during jump periods, and an ambulance with two medics is on standby. This is the domain of the jumpmasters and their boss, a Basque *adjudant-chef* known as *l'Ours* (the bear). The "bear" is a husky perfectionist with a sense of humor. He is also extremely serious about his work. His monitors put the new recruits of the *promo* (jump class) through their paces, supervise their physical training, and oversee their morale.

"The monitor is the first person of authority they see," the *adjudant-chef* explains, "and the last person they forget. After all, jumping is not normal. If it were, we'd have wings." The month's training on the ground concludes with a week of qualification jumps from an aircraft.

"Refusals to jump are rare," *l'Ours* confides, "About one or two maximum during a year. We have discussions, if there is a problem. After all, they *are* two time volunteers."

The regiment is proud of its low accident rate of less than one percent. The most common *"Bo-bos,"* or injuries, are muscular shocks, sprains, and ankle and knee breaks. To avoid finger and hand fractures, the jumpmasters warn their trainees not to attempt to break a fall with their hands. The calmest days sometimes produce the most injuries because the jumpers tend to relax or to become careless.

The 2nd REP is also proud of its speed record in emptying an aircraft of paras. A jumpmaster from another parachute regiment on temporary duty with the 2nd REP almost found himself airborne when he tried to slow a "stick" of Legionnaires hurrying toward the exit door like a clattering, many-legged caterpillar. The proximity of the DZ to the camp's buildings and the inevitable pilot errors resulting in early or late drops have occasionally brought jumpers crashing down on the barracks and camp buildings. The highest roofs are ringed with iron railings to keep paras or equipment from sliding off the tiles onto the ground.

A "stick" of ten recruits under the orders of a monitor is undergoing ground instruction at the edge of the DZ. The monitor, a fit, no-nonsense sergeant from Britain, is watching his men equip themselves for a theoretical jump. Stacked dorsal and ventral chutes are passed out by a corporal. The Legionnaires line the chutes up on the ground and place their helmets on them. At an order from the monitor, they don the helmets and chutes, checking buckles, straps, and static line hooks. They help one another and inspect their comrade's chute before signaling their readiness. Some of the apprentice paras seem to be lagging, and the sergeant tells them to hurry. *"En vitesse,"* he orders, before stepping forward to inspect their work. He pays special attention to the leg straps that can damage a man's testicles if not properly tightened. His OK is signaled by a hard slap on the dorsal chute, the jumpmaster's gesture of approval before an actual jump.

All Legionnaires take special care of their weapons, but a Legion para handles the parachutes he will be using with an equal amount of care. The billowing cloth canopy that allows him to drift safely to earth is a unique piece of equipment. Legion paras must spend a month in the parachute preparation hangar at Camp Raffalli. Thirty parachutes a day are folded and packed in this large building with its tall windows and long work tables. While one stack of parachutes is waiting to be processed, another contains those already packed. Each chute passes through four control phases to eliminate the possibility of error or shoddy work, each phase is recorded on paper and signed by those involved and the supervisor. The drying room next door to the hangar is a square, tower-like edifice with a powerful hot air blower that dries the rows of parachutes that hang like huge bats from the ceiling.

The repair facility is not far from the hangar and the drying room. It contains five large, heavy-duty sewing machines. An attractive female sergeant of the French Army with grey-flecked hair leads a small team of women specialists, on detached duty with the Legion, repairing the rips, tears, and strains the parachutes suffer from constant usage. The sergeant and her specialists, respected by the paras, are considered part of the Legion team during their assignment. There is always cold beer, lemonade, or hot coffee on hand in the repair shop and a bit of easy hospitality. A few days after my visit, while observing an airdrop from a Transall, I noted a surprisingly diminutive para among the stick that had just been ordered to stand and hook-up. A closer look identified the sergeant from the repair facility. I was later told that she felt it her duty to jump with the paras for as long as she was in charge of repairing their parachutes.

Once the apprentice paras have completed six jumps—including one at night—they are considered qualified and ready to receive their silver parachute wings. They will have to perform a minimum of six jumps a year, regardless of their assignment, to maintain their qualification. The presentation of the *brevet de parachutiste* takes place with the newly qualified jumpers in ranks before the headquarters building at Camp Raffalli. Either the commanding officer or his deputy normally presides over the ceremony. Other ranking officers pin on the shiny wings and affix the coveted *fourragère* of the Legion of Honor to the graduates' left shoulder. The ceremony is normally followed with a celebratory "*pot*," or drinks party, where the graduates are congratulated by senior officers and the jumpmasters who have seen them through their training. Later, they might visit Calvi to show off their new distinction. As one officer put it, "Now they roll their shoulders twice. Once for the *brevet*, and once for the *fourragère*."

If Camp Raffalli, its ordered barracks and planted areas, is now an established home for the 2nd REP, the return of the 2nd BEP to Algeria from Indochina on November 18, 1955, was fraught with uncertainty. Internal Army politics had almost resulted in the breakup of the 2nd BEP and an end to any possibility that the battalion would become a regiment in the existing reorganization.

The standing plan called for the formation of two parachute regiments in Algeria, the 1st and 3rd REP, with the 2nd BEP supplying the needed replacements. Fortunately for the 2nd BEP, Major George Masselot, an Indochina veteran, was a competent infighter when it came to military bureaucracy. In a comparatively short time, moving in and out of channels, and using his personal contacts, he managed to convince General Jean Gilles, the commander of French Airborne Forces, that the 2nd BEP should become the 2nd REP.

On December 1, 1955, the *2ème Régiment Étranger de Parachutistes* was created at Philippeville (now Skikda), Algeria, and the 3rd REP was dissolved. The Legion was thus able to provide two parachute regiments, the 1st and 2nd REPs—comrades-in-arms from the Indochina campaigns—for the spreading conflict in Algeria.

Clausewitz's truism about war, diplomacy, and politics took on a special meaning in Algeria. Although the Algerian war would approach and, in some situations, go beyond the Prussian strategist's definition of total war, it was a unique struggle that destroyed old rules and invented new procedures. This was no war between nation states, decided by climactic battles and ending in a flourish of gilt-edged diplomacy. It was a confusing mix of colonial collapse, nationalism, resentment, revenge, obstinacy, political extremes, heroism, betrayal, brutality, and lack of vision.

Most French *colons* in Indochina had held on to their lands and prerogatives until the end. Unless they were major plantation or mine owners, however, their role in exerting pressure on the military was minimal. The situation in Algeria was slightly different. The *pieds-noirs* (from the black boots worn by the first *colons*) of Algeria were the descendents of early French settlers who had established huge estates, vineyards, businesses, and farms. They were often the mayors and officials of the cities and towns. French politicians of various parties and government officials had repeatedly told them that Algeria was a Department of France and would remain so. They believed these promises and welcomed the army as their protector.

But most of the French-Algerians and their locally settled compatriots of Italian and Spanish ancestry wanted the army to protect their families, properties, and investments, preferably from static, defensive positions. They wanted them to be permanently on-the-spot as a reassuring, dissuasive presence. The arrival of the paras from Indochina and the development of mobile, helicopter-borne operations against distant, organized FLN units left many *pieds-noirs* feeling abandoned in their farmhouses and at the mercy of local terrorist groups. This situation created civilian-military tensions that would continue throughout the war.

The French Army was determined to win this war that had so many tactical parallels with the lost struggle in Vietnam. It was basically a guerrilla war, a blend of sudden terrorist attacks and small-unit actions; ambushes, hit-and-run operations and large, classic sweeps in search of rebel forces.

Despite the lessons of Indochina, the differences reappeared between the by-the-book conservative officers and those who wished to employ new methods and tactics. The paras were vocal in demanding more mobile operations and the means to implement them. The Legion paras again found themselves in the role of firemen, operating with other parachute units throughout Algeria.

The 2nd REP's records show the regiment in action in the Philippeville and Batna sectors. Later, in the Aurès mountain region, they participated in a "hard combat" at Ouled Fathma on April 30, 1956. In November 1956, the regiment was in Tebessa to operate along the Algerian-Tunisian border. There, it patrolled the frontier to block infiltration by the National Army of Liberation and to intercept arms shipments. The list of only a few of the regiment's violent encounters with the *Fellouze* reads like the map of Algeria: Mzran, Bir-El Ater, Dyr, Ben Djellal, Fedjoudi, Hamimat Guerra, El Milia, Souk Ahras.

The Algerian campaigns called for perseverance and constant physical exertion. The rebel regional units of the *Armée de Libération Nationale* (ALN) knew their territory. They took full advantage of the terrain, preparing dug-in, camouflaged positions for defense, frequently shifting locations, and attacking where and when the French were most vulnerable. French units with inexperienced draftees in their ranks were often targeted for attacks. In such situations, the paras of the Legion had to act as a relieving force or pursue the withdrawing rebels and attempt to cut them off. The clandestine political cells of the *Front de Libération Nationale* (FLN) guided the actions of the ALN and conducted their own deadly war in urban and rural areas.

Helicopter-borne operations increased as the war ground on. French majors and colonels learned to command from the air, watching an operation unfold on the ground, dropping in on company commanders to revise previous orders, or using their helicopter as an additional scout aircraft in seeking the enemy. The 2nd REP and its commanders helped write the book on chopper tactics, encirclement, and the rapid deployment of blocking forces. In Indochina, the French had used the chopper principally for Medevac and the transport of command groups. Some officers had even been criticized for suggesting its tactical use or employment as a gun platform. The situation changed in Algeria, where the chopper became a tactical workhorse.

But whether the paras reached some destinations by chopper, parachute, or truck, they often had to slog through burning Sahara sand, move through boot-tearing rock falls, or climb the snow-lashed heights of the Aurès in search of an elusive enemy. No matter what the preparation or caution, violent contact often came as a jolting suprise.

Sitting at his workplace in the cool wine cellars of the Legion retirement home at Puyloubier, former *Caporal-Chef* Sabatier recalled receiving a serious wound in the Aurès mountains in 1957.

"A *Fellagha* (rebel soldier) jumped from a hole in front of me and opened fire with an 8mm Beretta," Sabatier explains, rolling up his sleeve to show me how the first bullet shattered his arm, leaving it shorter than the other. A second bullet went through his wrist and a third blew off two fingers. "Two other bullets," he recalls, "lodged in the ammunition clip I was carrying in my belt. If not for the clip, they would have been fatal." A medic who came to Sabatier's aid was also hit before the "*Fell*" was killed by other Legionnaires.

While the 2nd REP continued its operations in Algeria, its sister regiment, the 1st REP, was joining other French Army units in preparation for the ill-fated Suez campaign. The Anglo-French-Israeli operation in early November 1956 was designed to topple the regime of Egyptian president Gamal Abdel Nasser. Nasser had nationalized the Suez Canal and was seen to pose a direct threat to Israel and the stability of the Middle East. The French armed forces were particularly eager to strike at Egypt, a nation they accused of supplying diplomatic and material assistance to the Algerian rebels. The 1st REP, jumping over Port Said on November 5, quickly subdued Egyptian resistance and secured the port. But U.S. and Soviet diplomatic protests and pressure brought the Suez operation to a halt within forty hours and hastened the withdrawal of the disgruntled French and British forces.

Meanwhile, the 2nd REP participated in several major combats in Algeria. An assault on an enemy position on the heights of Ahrour-el-Kifene resulted in 193 ALN dead and more than one hundred arms seized.

Excerpts from a declassified report on Operation "*Orléans*" of December 9, 1957, in the region of Djebel Fedjoudj reveals the importance of intelligence information and the planning and organizational effort required.

> "INTELLIGENCE: according to information initially furnished by a rebel prisoner captured on 10/22 (Sergeant H.L.L. of the 4th Company NAHIA of AIN BEIDA) and double-checked several times by intelligence sources and air observation, it appears that *Djebel Fedjoudj* is serving as a base for rebel units of the MINTAQUA 4: Companies of NAHIA of AIN BEIDA (4th Co.—3rd Co.) and AIN M'AILA (1st Co.).

"These rebel units probably returned to DJEBEL FEDJOUDJ soon after the engagement of 10/17/57 and were still there on 11/20. Each Company is composed of 3 platoons, each armed with 2 automatic weapons (automatic rifle or machine gun). In the last 2 weeks the 4th Company is said to have received 2 81mm mortars (it already has a 50mm mortar).

"A dissident band of OULED BENI MELLOUL, FROM FEDJOUDJ (about one Platoon with automatic weapons) must be added to the strength of these 3 Companies. Considering these reports and with the agreement of the neighboring Sector Commanders, the Colonel commanding the Sector of AIN has decided to launch an operation on 12/9/57 on the Djebel FEDJOUDJ and KEF SEFFANE.

The operational commander then issued orders to surround the area rapidly with three heliborne companies of the 2nd REP on the west slope, armored units on the north, south, and east slopes. Another company of the 2nd REP, a platoon of a Dragoon (Armor) Regiment, and two companies of the 8th Colonial Parachute Regiment formed the reserve force. Air and artillery support was augmented by the heavy weapons company of the 2nd REP with its 120mm and 81mm mortars and recoilless rifles.

The chopper lift began at 0856. At 1100 a Piper reconnaissance aircraft was hit by ground fire and spotted a group of rebels. From that moment, the slopes of the DJEBEL FEDJOUDJ became a small-scale battlefield. Artillery pounded suspect areas, strafing aircraft roared over the cuts and draws, and choppers lifted the Legion paras closer to the enemy. By 1300, the 2nd company was involved in a sharp firefight at a cost of one killed and two wounded. At 1400, some Legionnaires searched the *talweg* (valley) southwest of Hill 1200, while others scoured the hills. The last contact took place at 1600, and by 1850 the involved units were returning to their encampments.

The official *bilan* (score) of operation "*Orléans*," recorded with an overused typewriter ribbon, outlines a day of sweat, fear, risk, and loss presented as a bloodless balance sheet.

Friendly losses
    Personnel
        Killed: 1 (Sergent-Chef)
        Wounded: 5 (Caporal-Chef, Caporal, 3 Legionnaires)
Rebel losses
    Personnel
        Killed: 69 dead counted
        Prisoner: 1
    Armament: 1 Automatic Rifle   27 Rifles   6 Hunting Rifles
                    4 Submachine Guns   1 Automatic Pistol
                    1 Replacement barrel (MG)   12 Mortar Rounds
                    1 Light Mortar   1 Machine gun belt

The parallels with Indochina could be disconcerting. The Algerian members of the National Liberation Front appeared just as determined as their Vietminh counterparts. The writer and ex-Legion officer, Pierre Sergent, has described a Vietminh ruse the "Fell" used in Algeria. In 1959, after surrounding a well-armed group of rebels south of Bône, near *l'oued Seybouse,* the companies of the 2nd REP were astounded to find the enemy had disappeared into thin air. It took Major Cabiro, a survivor of Dien Bien Phu and legendary para, to solve the mystery. After surveying the calm water of *l'oued* (flooded wadi), he decided the rebels might be hidden under the surface and breathing through reeds, much as their Asian counterparts had breathed through bamboo or reeds in Indochina.

After ordering his men to grenade the stream, he soon found his hunch was correct. An entire ALN unit floundered from the water, trying to escape the grenading. Twenty-nine rebels were killed and ten were taken prisoner. An automatic rifle, fourteen submachine guns, and twenty-three rifles were captured. Most important, three high-powered radio sets meant to provide contact between ALN units in the Kabylia mountains and rebel bases in Tunisia were recovered. It could be that one of the dead Algerians hiding in *l'oued Seybouse* had learned the reed trick in Indochina while fighting under the French flag. If so, the fickle fortunes of war had brought him together with Cabiro for a fatal meeting.

At the beginning of the Algerian War, the rebels had been armed haphazardly with hunting rifles, shotguns, and weapons captured from the French. With the cold war heating up, the Eastern Bloc nations and China recognized the West's vulnerability to revolutionary warfare. Modern arms and munitions were soon filtering across Algeria's borders from Tunisia and Morocco.

The FLN political structure and the ALN command were often plagued with infighting and rivalry. This increased their vulnerability to French intelligence operations. Regardless, small bands of rebels, once surrounded, often fought to the death. Englishman and author Simon Murray, who served in the 2nd REP during the Algerian War, described such an engagement in his book on his five years in the French Foreign Legion:

> We shot it out with the fell [*sic*] all afternoon—rifle barrels boiling and Sten guns sizzling. Two dive-bombers came to our assistance and hammered the gorge with rockets and napalm, all to no avail—the Arabs never stopped firing. Choppers circled overhead and ceaselessly machine-gunned the Arab positions without success. The Arab side of the gorge became a flaming hell and it was incredible that they could continue to live in it. But they did, and defiantly responded to every bomb with a blast of machine-gun fire.

Although the Indochina War had its share of brutality, the savagery of the Algerian conflict was both impressive and infectious. Terrorists of the FLN placed deadly bombs in the crowded milk bars, cafes, cinemas, and dance halls of Algiers and other cities and towns, creating carnage among both French and Algerian civilians. Algerians and their families, accused of "collaborating" with the French, be they civilian officials, businessmen, journalists, or even laborers, risked having their throats slit (the "Kabylie smile"). Others had their noses, ears, or lips sliced off as macabre, living warnings to others.

Some French law enforcement officers, intelligence officials, and units of the Army fought fire with fire. FLN and ALN captives and suspects suffered beatings, torture, and occasional summary execution, depending upon the circumstances of their capture and their revolutionary role.

Because of the profound effect the Algerian War had on the Foreign Legion—and the 2nd REP—it is necessary to highlight certain events of the conflict and to explain their significance.

The 10th Parachute Division under the command of Gen. Jacques Massu was ordered into the city of Algiers in 1957 to reestablish order and crush the active terrorist cells of the FLN. The 1st REP, along with other non-Legion paras was thus actively involved in the ten-month "Battle of Algiers." This eventual "victory" broke the back of the FLN cells in the city. It was tarnished, however, by the use of torture during the interrogation of FLN prisoners.

Some officers justified electric shock treatment from a manually activated generator. They claimed the information and confessions obtained were invaluable in saving innocent lives, capturing FLN operatives, and foiling future terrorist attacks. Other officers resigned their commissions in protest, arguing that such methods were staining the army's honor. A public debate on torture became a political hot potato in France, dividing the nation even more on the pursuit of the Algerian War.

Fortunately for the 2nd REP, its units were far from Algiers, operationally involved in the *bled*, or countryside, on search-and-destroy missions. The regiment's highly successful actions along the electrified barrier fence of the *Ligne Morice* on the Tunisian border were causing heavy ALN casualties.

By late 1959, the 2nd REP, as the spearhead unit of the Eastern Zone, had participated in a long series of operations named "Precious Stones." The success of these and other French operations was creating a paradox. Militarily, the French were winning the war. In Paris and internationally, it was being lost. Public opinion in France had turned against government policy. Draftees were refusing service in Algeria, and the political Left was encouraging desertion. Although the ALN had suffered grievous losses in the field, some of the FLN's urban political cells were managing to reconstitute themselves. General deGaulle's return to power in 1958 and his two trips to Algeria that year had raised vain hopes among the military and the *pieds noirs* for more understanding and support from the Paris government.

Had not the tall presence of deGaulle shouting "I have understood you" and "Long Live French Algeria" produced wild elation among the crowds at the *Place du Forum* in Algiers? The enthusiasm of the *pieds noirs* and the army, however, had been brief. In 1959, deGaulle launched a series of secret and public diplomatic approaches to the FLN seeking an end to the conflict based on some form of self-determination for Algeria.

Such proposals were anathema to the army, which felt betrayed—as though its past sacrifices had been ignored. General Massu declared publicly that he and his officers would not "execute unconditionally the orders of the Head of State." He was immediately ordered back to Paris for a dressing-down and reassigned, but the match he had struck had fallen on dry tinder. In January 1960, militant *pieds noirs* launched antigovernment street demonstrations in Algiers and fired on troops of the National Gendarmerie. Ominously, nearby paras of the 1st REP, sympathetic to the cause of French Algeria, did not intervene.

The seeds of rebellion continued to flourish in the overheated political climate of Algiers. On April 22, 1961, four French generals—Maurice Challe, commander in chief in Algeria; retired Gen. Raoul Salan, former commander in chief in both Algeria and Indochina; Edmond Jouhaud, Air Force Chief of Staff; and André Zeller, retired Armed Forces Chief of Staff attempted what became known as "the Generals Putsch." It was of particular significance to the Legion that its inspector general, Gen. Paul Gardy, joined the rebellion. The objective was to defy deGaulle's government, topple it, and keep Algeria French. The 1st REP was among the first active units to support the rebel generals.

Returning to Philippeville from operations, the 2nd REP found confusion and a spate of rumors. The paras of the 2nd REP were surprised to learn that their sister regiment had taken over the city of Algiers, its government buildings, and radio station. That night, after Lt. Colonel Darmuzai, the regimental commander, had turned in, Major Cabiro, with the agreement of Colonel Brechignac, the Divisional Chief of Staff, defied Darmuzai's instructions to sit tight and led the 2nd REP to Algiers.

The puzzled Legion paras found themselves being greeted like liberators by the *pieds noirs,* as they drove into the city. Ordered to secure the airport, they drove off a defending force of French Marines, using sharpened wooden posts as weapons. Unbriefed by their officers and unsure of their objectives, some Legionnaires resented being treated like military automatons. It became clear, however, that they might soon be involved in an antigovernment airdrop on Paris in support of a genuine coup d'état.

DeGaulle had other ideas. Appearing on national television in his old wartime uniform of a brigadier general, he delivered a blistering indictment of the rebel generals, demanded the support of the army, and called upon the citizens of France for help. Stationed in Marseille at the time as the chief of the USIA office and a U.S. Consul, I had watched deGaulle's performance with particular interest. I had experienced the bitter anti-American feelings of the French in Saigon as they withdrew from Indochina. I was also well aware that certain right-wing elements and *pieds noirs* circles in Marseille were already blaming the United States for the situation in Algeria. The thought of my old para companions from Indochina arriving in France as pawns in an illegal, right-wing *Algérie Française* takeover was a frightening prospect.

I need not have worried. DeGaulle's appeal struck a cord with the French population. Many ambivalent individuals suddenly realized the seriousness of the situation. DeGaulle, always the master politician, had delivered a moving performance that snuffed the flame of revolt like a sudden, cold wind.

"The evening has come," Simon Murray wrote of his wait at the Algiers Airport for the transport aircraft that never appeared with a certain tongue-in-cheek resignation. "A kind of stalemate appears to have been reached. DeGaulle has brought up tanks in France and threatened to shoot parachutists out of the air if a drop is made. This has dampened some of yesterday's thoughts of dancing in Paris and put prospects of dinner at Maxim's tomorrow night slightly further away."

By April 26, 1961, it was all over. The key leaders of the revolt had fled, and the 1st REP's days were numbered. The Legionnaires of the 1st REP had blown up their solidly constructed barracks at Zeralda before being trucked off to Sidi-bel-Abbès, where the regiment would be officially disbanded and struck from the rolls of the French Army. As the trucks swung onto the main road, the disgruntled paras sang Edith Piaf's "Je ne regrette rien" (I regret nothing) as a symbolic act of defiance.

Meanwhile, the 2nd REP, trucked back to Philippeville after playing a "fringe" role in the revolt, found itself barred from its own base at Camp Pehaut and ordered to erect tents two miles distant in the nearby hills. By May 3, 1961, the regiment was back on operation in the Aurès Mountains but its future and the future of the entire Legion was very much in doubt.

3

A REGIMENT SURVIVES

Schwitzen spart Blut—Sweat saves blood.

A Legion justification for hard training.

Marseille was bright and sunny on July 14, 1961. The mistral wind buffeted the crowd lining the sidewalks along the Canebière and riffled the waters of the Vieux Port. The traditional Bastille Day parade that year was unique. Word had gone out that it might be the Legion's last appearance in the port city, and many Marseillais had come to say a personal good-bye. The dissolution of the 1st REP was said to have been only the beginning. Other regimental flags were soon expected to be on their way to the museum of the Legion. The parliamentary Left was advocating that the "mercenaries" be struck from the state's payroll. Rumor had it that *le Grand Charles,* for his own reasons, had decided the matter. The Foreign Legion, according to some media commentators, would soon belong to history.

The parade that day featured regular army, navy, and air force units as well as the respected firemen of Marseille. It had almost reached its climax when a gap appeared in the line of march. A bemused silence settled on the crowd. Then, to a growing, anticipatory hum, the notes of "Le Boudin," the Legion's march, and the sound of handclapping echoed from the buildings lining the broad avenue. The white képis of the bearded, leather-aproned Legion sappers came into view, and the crowd began cheering. They were followed by the Legion infantry. Grim-faced, arms swinging to the pace of their traditional slow march, the tanned, much decorated Legionnaires kept their eyes forward without acknowledging the many shouts of "*Vive la Légion.*" If it were a last parade, it was also a moving farewell. More than one handkerchief was in use as the Marseillais bid their Legionnaires "adieu."

Later, rationalizing the crowd's reaction, I realized there was more to it than a fondness for a corps that had been a part of the city's history for so

35

long. By cheering the Legion, some of the Marseillais were expressing their disapproval of deGaulle and his policies. Others, aware that the loss of Algeria would mean many changes and trials ahead, were moved to tears by regret as much as by the possible dissolution of the Legion. For the elderly, the impending demise of the Legion was another rip in the tapestry of their life, signaling unwelcome change.

Under the circumstances, it was not difficult to understand deGaulle's negative attitude. The instances during World War II when Legionnaires obeyed their French officers, who, in turn, followed the orders of the Vichy government, were undoubtedly still fresh in his mind. The armed opposition by certain Legion units to the Allied landings in North Africa when deGaulle was struggling to gain Allied acceptance for his Free French forces must have been particularly infuriating for the proud general. The fact that these foreigners, serving under the French flag, had now attempted to overthrow the French Republic and foil his plans to end the Algerian War had been totally unacceptable.

Fortunately for the Legion and for the 2nd REP, fate and politics had placed an influential advocate in the deGaulle Cabinet. Pierre Messmer, the stolid minister of defense, had served with the Legion as a captain in the 13th demibrigade during World War II. Although the real give-and-take over whether the Legion should live or die will probably never be revealed, Messmer could well have reminded deGaulle that the men of Messmer's own 13th DBLE had fought with distinction as members of the Free French forces at Bir Hakeim and El Ghazala in the western desert—at a time when deGaulle sorely needed such performances. Whatever the discussion or argument, the guillotine did not fall, and the Legion was reprieved.

Although the rebel generals had been crushed, and the deGaulle government was moving toward a negotiated settlement of the Algerian conflict, there was much bitterness and growing unrest in France. The fate of Algeria and its *pieds noirs* population was a constant concern, as was the state of the army, its morale, and effectiveness. The officers and men who had survived Indochina were aware that they might soon be asked to abandon the Algerian comrades-in-arms serving by their side, as they had been forced to leave their Vietnamese, Cambodian, and Laotian allies in 1955.

In Algeria, the 2nd REP mirrored the malaise and uncertainty about the future that was felt by other Legion units. Many of its officers had been relieved of their duties to appear before military courts. The feeling was that the Legion had been apportioned too much blame for the recent events, and doubts existed concerning the future conduct of the ongoing war. Professional or not, few soldiers relish becoming a target when they know a conflict is winding down.

Lt. Colonel Darmuzai—who had railed against his rebellious officers and threatened them with a firing squad—had turned the regiment over to his replacement, Lt. Colonel Maurice Chenel, on May 4, 1961. Chenel was a Legionnaire of the old school, an Indochina veteran, and an alumnus of Dien Bien Phu. Although he had recently qualified as a para, he had never commanded an airborne unit. From the day of his takeover until July 2, 1962, the day Algeria became independent, Chenel had made sure the 2nd REP did not vegetate. He had also kept them away from the cities and possible contact with *pieds noirs* linked to the OAS (*l'Organization de l'Armée Secrète*). This clandestine organization, led by renegade French generals, was attempting to recruit disgruntled Legionnaires for its terrorist campaign against the deGaulle government. When the 2nd REP was not on operations in the region of Constantine, Chenel had kept it sweating over building projects. Those Legionnaires who cursed their commander for unproductive operations and make-work projects did not fully understand his motivation. The 2nd REP was still under suspicion for both the known anti-Gaullist sympathies of some of its officers and the regiment's unauthorized trip to Algiers in support of the putsch. Aware that there were some in the army who would like to see the 2nd REP disbanded, Chenel was protecting the regiment and ensuring its longevity by keeping it isolated and fully occupied. This busy period also kept both officers and men from brooding over their inevitable departure from Algeria and the abandonment of the cradle of the Legion at Sidi-bel-Abbès.

A retired German *adjudant-chef* who had lived through this period with the 2nd REP phrased it succinctly. "Chenel was determined to ensure that order and discipline reigned. He decided to put the regiment to work on roads, bridges, and buildings to save it from dissolution. Don't try to glorify the regiment," he cautioned me, "All of our (the Legion's) units are equally good." Earlier, when I'd encouraged him to speak of his own adventures in Algeria, Gabon, and Central Africa, he had simply replied, "I have nothing to say."

On July 2, 1962, Algeria became independent. The *fellagha* of the ALN and the officials of the FLN left their mountain redoubts or crossed the border from their safe havens in Tunisia or Morocco to establish a presence in Algerian cities and towns. It was a difficult period. Over six years of brutal warfare and losses had left raw nerves and a legacy of hate on both sides. Legionnaire Simon Murray described the atmosphere at the time.

> Too much hatred has been produced over these last years for it to be erased by the signing of a document of peace. Revenge is human. When we left Philippe-ville, a small unit remained behind to do the final clearing up. On the last night two legionnaires were attacked in Philippeville. One got away, the other was decapitated.

French Army units were withdrawing from Algeria and taking a number of *Harki* (loyal Algerian irregulars) with them. The killing continued as rival

FLN factions battled for supremacy. A hunt with fatal consequences had begun for those Algerians who had cooperated with the French. Isolated in their barracks at Telergma, the men of the 2nd REP pondering their 824 dead in Indochina, their 233 dead in Algeria, and all their wounded in both wars, were wondering about the future.

In late August, the 2nd REP was ordered to the town of Bou Sfer to provide security for the French Naval base of Mers El Kebir near Oran. Under the terms of the Evian Accords, the base would remain in French hands for an unspecified period. At Bou Sfer, with the war ended, the pick and shovel took priority over the rifle and the grenade. The Legionnaire's reputation as builders was put to the test once again. Alloted an inhospitable camp terrain that threatened to become a swamp with the first rains, the parachutists of the 2nd REP, according to former para and author Pierre Sergent, turned into "diggers, masons, carpenters, and plumbers . . ."

These physical efforts may have kept the paras occupied and provided them with a certain satisfaction in the final result, but the 2nd REP was not meant to be a regiment of laborers. As the only parachute regiment left to the Legion, it had inherited a proud tradition, but a military organization cannot survive on tradition alone. It must have a clearly defined purpose as well as the motivation and means to implement its assigned missions. Just as uncertainty and lethargy became the norm at Bou Sfer, the Legion's inherent gift for renewal and self-preservation came to the fore.

The catalyst for this positive change was Lt. Colonel Robert Caillaud, a distinguished parachute officer and veteran of World War II and Indochina with a taste for, and understanding of, unconventional warfare. When Caillaud took command of the 2nd REP in late May 1963, Lt. Colonel Chenel had accomplished his difficult mission. The 2nd REP had retained its integrity and the voices of those crying for its dissolution had been muted if not stilled.

When the new commander addressed the assembled officers to explain his plans for the future, his speech had the effect of a thunderbolt. Not only would they be operational paras again, but they would also be part of a very special regiment. Lt. Colonel Caillaud was looking ahead to the demands of the cold war and a world of postcolonial unrest. He was not looking back at the past and the traditional, large-scale deployment of airborne formations in set piece battles. Nor, he made it clear, should his officers continue to mull over the recent events in Algeria. He asked them to look to the future. He wanted the 2nd REP to be ready for any mission, anywhere, no matter how difficult, no matter how dangerous, varied, or unusual. The more Caillaud explained, the more enthusiastic his audience became. It was as though they were suddenly shedding the dusty role of work-site overseers and returning to their true calling as operational paras.

A veteran of special warfare and commando operations, Caillaud had drawn on his knowledge of foreign special operations forces, including the British Special Air Service (SAS) to develop his plans. These plans called for the regiment to undergo radical change. A jump school at Calvi, Corsica, would be established to train an elite team of operational jumpers. Each of the four combat companies would have specialized skills and tasks:

- 1st Company: intelligence gathering, operations behind enemy lines, deep penetration patrols;
- 2nd Company: mountain warfare, including formation of ski scouts;
- 3rd Company: amphibious operations, including subaqua infiltration, combat swimmers;
- 4th Company: mine warfare and sniping.

This was a revolutionary concept at the time and not one to please desk-bound conservatives in the French military. To these officers the word "special" conjured up nonconforming, rogue units. The same mentality in more recent times led their Pentagon counterparts to label U.S. Special Forces "snake eaters" and to shortchange the budget for Special Operation Forces.

Fortunately for Colonel Caillaud, the Foreign Legion had always been semi-independent. When preparing the research plan for this book, I asked an information officer of the regular army in Paris about the necessary official clearances.

"Oh," he'd shrugged, indicating with a wave that such things were not within his authority, "The Legion is the Legion."

Although Caillaud had received support for his plan from his superiors, installing the new regime, scraping together specialist training personnel, equipment, and—above all—funds, would not be easy. But the Legion has always had a particular expertise for "unofficial requisitions" and the profitable use of networking between officers, warrant officers and noncoms. Legionnaires of the 2nd REP, considered past masters of the *"systeme D"* for *"de-merder"* (get oneself out of the s. . .) or—in more polite terms—of being resourceful, pulled out all the stops. Established friendships with the French Navy were invaluable in obtaining equipment, organizing landing exercises, and establishing the regiment's amphibious capabilities. Contacts forged as cadets at Saint Cyr with officers now serving in the *Chasseurs Alpins* were useful in seeking advice and assistance in the preparations for mountain warfare training. Some regimental cadre were sent to Commando School, others to air-ground support courses. Legion personnel files were combed for experts on demolition, sniping, survival, house-to-house fighting, and hand-to-hand combat, and requests were made for their transfer to the 2nd REP.

Simon Murray, returning to the regiment after successfully completing the required training course for his corporal's stripes found a "hive of activity."

"Everybody," he recalled, "seems to be undergoing some kind of specialist training." He was surprised to find "a frogman unit . . . which appears to be professional in the way it operates and in its results." He learned that forty men had been sent to a ski training school in France to form an Alpine unit. A three week, night-warfare course was teaching the paras to operate exclusively at night. Landings from submarine and rubber dinghies, and a rigorous, dangerous course in antitank warfare were all part of the regiment's new look.

By the time the first advance group of the 2nd REP had arrived at Calvi in December 1963 under the command of Major de Biré, another *ancien* of Dien Bien Phu, Colonel Caillaud had succeeded with an unusual coup. The French Army's Airborne Command at Pau had agreed to allow the Legion its own jump school at Calvi where the 2nd REP's recruits could become parachute qualified. Later, the regiment would use the Legion's Commando Training Center at Mont Louis in the Pyrénées for more specialization. Major de Biré moved his officers and men into the old Citadel and the former jump center of the "Shock" regiments at the Camp of Fiume-Secco. He went to work with his usual despatch, and soon each company of the regiment was being introduced to Corsica under a three-month rotation plan.

In June 1967, the 2nd REP, the last French combat unit to leave Algeria, was transferred to Calvi and installed at Fiume-Secco. On the occasion of Camerone 1968, the Camp of Fiume-Secco was renamed after Major Raffalli.

The 2nd REP also became a part of the French Army's 11th Parachute Division and an on-call member of France's Rapid Action Force (FAR) whose slogan is "Fast, Strong, and Far."

In addition to the 2nd REP, the 11th Parachute Division includes four Regiments of Marine Infantry (RPIMA), two Regiments of Chasseurs Parachutists (RCP), one Regiment of Parachute Hussars (RHP), one Regiment of Parachute Artillery (RAP), one Regiment of Parachute Engineers (RGP), a Command & Service Regiment (RPCS), and a Mobile Operational Airborne Base (BOMAP).

Thanks to Colonel Caillaud and his successors, the regiment was no longer solely a traditional unit of parachute infantry. It was to become what Bruce Quarrie in his book, "The World's Elite Forces," describes as "an extraordinary flexible air-commando regiment."

The innovations pioneered by Caillaud and his staff have been refined and updated over the years depending on changes in tactics and equipment, the lessons learned in training, and on actual combat operations. The continued importance of flexibility and innovation is stressed by Lt. Colonel Rideau, the 2nd REP's current operations officer with an unofficial motto: "Can do—Can change."

Today the responsibilities and tasks of each company have evolved depending on new tactics and operational needs. A Command and Service Company

(CCS) staffs the Regimental Command Post, handles communications, personnel, security, logistics, health, and other administrative duties, and maintains a rear base when the regiment is on operation.

The Reconnaissance and Support Company (CEA) is made up of two platoons of MILAN Anti-tank Missiles, a platoon of heavy (120mm) mortars, a platoon of 20mm rapid fire antiaircraft guns, and a jeep-mounted reconnaissance platoon. A team of *Commandos de Recherche et d'Action dans le Profondeur,* bearing the unfortunate acronym *"CRAP,"* and charged with information-gathering and deep-penetration actions, is integrated into the CEA. This team of *chuteurs opérationnels,* expert at HALO (high altitude-low opening) drops, gives the regiment a unique reconnaissance and intelligence capability.

The Legionnaires of the 1st Company have maintained their original role as *"croquers des chars"* (tank crunchers) and experts at night operations. They learn to remain calm as heavy tank treads roll over their narrow-mouthed foxholes or when they steady an 89 mm LRAC (antitank rocket launcher) on a tank heading hell-for-leather in their direction. Like their predecessors in Indochina, they have learned that proper training and practice can make an ally of the night, providing them with anonymity and rendering an enemy vulnerable.

The men of the 1st Company have broadened their expertise in other fields. Action at Kolwezi, Zaire, and operations in Beirut, Somalia, and Sarajevo have taught the 2nd REP the importance of mastering urban warfare, and the 1st has taken on the job. House-to-house fighting—one of the most difficult tasks faced by any infantry unit—requires a state of constant alert. In a combat environment where every doorway, roof, or window poses a possible threat, quick reactions and fast decisions are crucial "stay alive" factors. A simple street crossing, followed by an attack on a building or house, calls for precise procedures. Covering fire, previous selection of concealment and cover, blocking escape routes, and rapid entry techniques are but a few such considerations. A subspecialization in sniping fits into the company's urban warfare role. In the confusion, smoke, and dust of street warfare, the Legion's skilled two-man sniping teams can be invaluable.

A muscular noncom from the 2nd Company briefed me on the specialization of his unit. He and his comrades had undergone the same basic training as the *Chasseurs Alpins,* France's crack mountain troops. They had first passed through the Alpine training center at Chamonix in the French Alps which was followed by a year of advanced training at Barcelonnette during which they qualified as Alpine climbers and skiers. The two men best qualified in each category become training cadre.

The high Alps are about as far as one can get from the Legion's traditional home in the desert. The 2nd Company's equipment includes cross-country skis, telescoping metal poles, grappling hooks, white winter camouflage parkas, and all the accoutrements for climbing, including stout ropes, ice axes, and crampons.

"If you've come from the mountains," the noncom explained, "you'll end up in the 2nd Company." He described the special quality of the mountains hesitantly as though he did not expect an outsider to understand. "There's a certain attraction to the mountains, a unique ambiance," he explained. "Life in the company can be physically hard. The mountains do not give you a second chance. But the company gathers strength and pride from the hardships we endure—particularly when officers, noncoms, and Legionnaires are living together in extreme conditions."

The 2nd Company has its own MILAN capability, mortars, and a 20mm gun in support. The mountain environment poses particular problems when it comes to arms and equipment. Rations freeze easily. Individual weapons must be placed outside a shelter rather than be kept close to the body to avoid the condensation that would cause serious freezing. Legionnaires learn to survive in jagged, glacial landscapes, cutting snow holes for warmth and remaining alert to the threats of frostbite, snowblindness, and fatigue. Changing light, snowglare, winds, mountain shadows, and sudden storms change standard aiming and firing procedures. Accurate estimation of range and distance is difficult, and echoes or muffled sounds tend to disorient. Despite these hazards, I had the impression that the mountaineer I was interviewing would not have traded places with anyone in another company.

The 3rd Company, trained in one of the first regimental specialties, is responsible for the Amphibious Center at Camp Raffalli. This resort-like modern complex with slanting roofs is located on the beach. Concrete launching ramps on a calm river mouth provide access to the surf for the company's thirty-six inflatable Zodiacs powered by long-shaft Suzuki 40 hp engines. Wet suits hang on racks in the storage area, diving cylinders are aligned against the wall, and field radios and other pieces of equipment are stored nearby. There are sleeping and changing areas, offices, and a central room with a large fireplace—an amenity appreciated by returning swimmers during the winter months.

Although the beach and barbecue facilities of the center are sometimes open to Legion families during a good-weather weekend, the center is far from being a resort. Day or night, rain or shine, the Legionnaires of the 3rd Company spend most of their waking hours on or in the water. The current Chief of Recruitment for the Legion, Lt. Colonel Jacques Hogard, now based at

Aubagne, recalled his service with the 3rd as a lieutenant and captain from 1986 to 1988.

"The sea can be a hostile environment for combat swimmers," he explained. "The isolation or disorientation of individual swimmers during a long operation can be a real problem." He emphasized that the only antidote was a regular retraining program and cited a commandment of the Legion, "Hard Training—Easy War." I was able to appreciate this truism while observing the daily routine.

The men of the 3rd Company, clad in dark, tight-fitting wet suits, look appropriately like seals as they line up on the military side of Calvi airport to board a Transall for an early morning drop into the cold water of the bay. Peering from the balaclava-like helmets of their wet suits, they resemble knights wearing chain mail headpieces. When the stick of *nageurs* (swimmers) tumbles out of the aircraft, the bay below is covered with a wispy morning mist. Although Zodiacs are standing by in the event of accidents, the swimmers are on their own once they hit the water. The morning's effort involves a long swim to shore, pushing a flotation sack filled with equipment, followed by a beach-clearing exercise. Not all such deliveries are by parachute. Direct drops into sea, lake, or river without parachutes are often made from low-flying, momentarily hovering choppers.

Other operations might include surreptitious debarkation from a Navy submarine at some isolated point along the wild Corsican coastline. This could be followed by the subaqua infiltration of a river, using special "no bubble" scuba equipment, to gather information or to find a designated demolition target.

Company Adjudant (warrant officer) Zigic, a husky Serb with fifteen years' service in the 2nd REP, described the 3rd Company's training. "We start with someone who may have never swum before. He will eventually be capable of parachuting into a wet DZ, dropping from a chopper, or launching from a submarine or fast boat. He will be able to swim 14 kilometers at sea—day or night, mark a beach for assault landings, plant mines, infiltrate a river for several kilometers, and set charges. Regardless of his mission, he must be ready to fight at all times. He must also be an expert map reader and a handler of kayaks and Zodiacs."

On another day, the platoons of the 3rd Company are out on the heather-covered hills perfecting their markmanship on the firing ranges. The cool wind is acrid with the odor of gunpowder as the Legionnaires fire their 5.56mm FAMAS assault rifles, a modern weapon of "bullpup" design developed with the assistance of the German arms firm Heckler & Koch. The stubby rifle is nicknamed *Le Clarion* (the bugle) because of its unusual shape. The marksmen are aiming at silhouette targets, loosing fire in ripping bursts, raising plumes of dust from the butts. Firing ceases periodically, weapons are secured, and the noncoms go forward with marking crayons to record the hits.

A quarter of a mile distant, other marksmen are learning to fire the *Minimi*, a magazine fed, 5.56mm light machine gun, under the watchful eye of a thin lieutenant who is observing the impacts through binoculars. Cartridge cases glint in the sun as they spew from the guns and clatter onto a cement firing platform. A short distance away, over a rocky hill and down a narrow goat path, more Legionnaires are gripping MAB 9mm automatic pistols with both hands, emptying their magazines at stand-up targets. An indomitable song bird—silent during the firing—fills each cessation with his chirping.

As an old soldier and *ancien d'Indo,* I am allowed to try my hand at the unfamiliar weapons. The result is not inspiring. Although I manage five hits out of ten with the FAMAS—the equal of my officer escort—my showing with the *Minimi* is dismal. Maybe it was the light? I hesitate to mention the pistol results. Suffice it to say that it was no worse than my minimum qualification with a .45 automatic in 1943.

Thoroughly chastened, I drifted away from the earsplitting racket of the ranges to a group of Legionnaires sitting on a slight rise of brush-covered ground. Like soldiers the world over, they were taking advantage of a morning break to ease their hunger, spreading pâté from a ration tin on crusty hunks of bread. They watched me approach, a strange, bearded apparition in a bush hat, and nodded uncertain greetings. They had been speaking English.

"Where are you from?," I asked one of them.

"New Zealand," he replied.

"And you?"

"England."

"And yourself?" I asked, turning to the third Legionnaire.

"Ireland," he answered.

"Really?", I said surprised, "Where exactly in Ireland?"

"Kinsale," was the answer.

It was hard to believe. Deep in the Corsican *maquis,* amid the din of automatic weapons, I had found a Legionnaire from my own place of residence, a small harbor town on the south coast of Ireland. One of the sons of the local veterinary surgeon had decided to join the Legion. He had been in uniform for ten months, and he was due to receive his parachute qualification in a few weeks' time. He told me he had always wanted to be a soldier. I could only assure him he had made a good choice, if that was his desire. In a historical context, he was following a well-worn path. Many Irish had served the French kings as professional soldiers, particularly after the English victory at the Battle of Kinsale—outside his home town—in 1601.

I then came upon two noncoms concentrating on a small, unfamiliar piece of hand-held equipment. I soon learned that today's infantry patrols can ascertain their position accurately by satellite navigation with the Global Positioning System (GPS) in much the same way as a ship at sea. The only thing worrying the Legionnaires was the ultimate longevity of the American satellite providing the signal.

Back at Camp Raffalli, Captain Eric de Minieres, the company commander, received me in his office. A tall, soft-spoken man with a ready smile, he asked me to join him for an *apéro* (aperitif) in the "Club" housed in the company's barracks. Before we left the office, he proudly displayed a framed document marking the Legion's coordination with the U.S. Marine Corps in Mogadishu, Somalia, during the winter of 1993. The citation, signed by General Wilhelm, USMC, states in part, "We were honored and privileged to serve shoulder-to-shoulder with you and your superb company."

The 4th Company is specially trained to operate behind enemy lines and to create selective havoc in its path. The Legionnaires of the 4th Company are the expert marksmen and *destructeurs*, demolition experts, of the regiment. They follow in the tradition of the French Resistance (FFI), the British SOE (Special Operations Executive), and American OSS (Office of Strategic Services). Churchill told the SOE to "set Europe ablaze" during World War II, and the 4th Company's mission is much the same today in a different context. Their specialties are sabotage and deadly harassment, the cutting of communication lines, the use of mines and booby traps.

The company's snipers use a standard 7.26mm (NATO) scoped rifle and the huge, scoped, American Barrett .50-caliber precision rifle that can pierce light armor and walls at 1,800 meters distance. These marksmen train night and day in all conditions. They are masters of camouflage and accustomed to lying in ambush positions over long periods of time. They can operate alone or as two-man teams using special tactics to reveal, fix, and eliminate enemy targets. Serb snipers at Sarajevo learned to be wary of expert Legion marksmen. The newly formed 5th Company is responsible for the essential task of maintaining and repairing regimental equipment.

Another early morning start and a kidney-jarring jeep ride put me in a position to watch the MILAN teams of the CEA (Recon and Support Company) hump their thirty-six-pound weapons and twenty-four-pound missiles up a steep mountain slope. The MILAN (light antitank missile) is a highly effective, tripod-mounted weapon with a maximum range of 2,000 meters. It fires a wire-guided, hollow-charge missile that can pierce armor like a dart and generate heavy heat while ricocheting inside a tank turret. The MILAN can also penetrate two meters of cement and is useful against pillboxes.

This technical jargon was far from my thoughts, as I willed my breakfast to settle and watched the perspiring Legionnaires struggling with their loads. The whip aerials of some Peugeot jeeps marked a hillcrest PC. Another squad was preparing its weapons and missiles for airdrop in special containers, padding them to break the landing shock. Some supervising noncoms were timing the teams to see how quickly the preparation could be completed.

Owing to the constant threat of brush and forest fires, the MILAN teams are restricted to dry-firing in Corsica. Their live-fire training is conducted at Camp Canjuers, an extensive military reservation in southern France. Meanwhile, a MILAN *chef de section* and his team are building an indoor, electronic, simulated firing range at Camp Raffalli in an abandoned warehouse with materiel they can "appropriate."

Another group was gathered around a jeep crisscrossed with heavy canvas slings. A sergeant was tugging on the slings and readjusting them before giving a brief lecture.

"I'll tell you one thing," he snapped. "If this job isn't done properly, the jeep will swing or twirl when lifted. If it does, the pilot can justifiably drop the load to save his *helico*. If he does, your pay will go toward buying a new jeep." The warning is greeted with nervous smiles.

On the edge of the hillcrest, a British *caporal-chef* and medic is testing Legionnaires on their knowledge of first aid techniques to qualify for their lance-corporal's stripes. The exercise consists of removing a badly wounded man from a jeep and performing the necessary emergency treatment. The blond Legionnaire being tested is from eastern Europe and is so nervous he is almost hyperventilating. The medic tells him to relax, take his time, and think, before he responds to the questions. He does well on checking for broken bones, the need for mouth-to-mouth resuscitation, and the application of a tourniquet. He has to be reminded about promptly reporting the accident by radio, clearly presenting the facts, and—above all—giving the exact location of the accident. The Legionnaire acting as the injured party seems to be thoroughly enjoying his role, lying at ease in the sun with his eyes closed.

The memory of that first aid drill came dramatically to mind the next morning. Captain Patrice Valentin of the CEA, a tough, taciturn young officer, drove me high into the mountains off the main road to Saint Florent to join up with the company's heavy mortar platoon. The narrow track wound ever higher. From my side of the jeep, there were spectacular sheer drops onto the rocks below. I suspected the captain's family motto was *toujours l'audace* (always daring) because he drove like a fearless cavalryman. Occasionally, as we sped over the rocky road, he would take one hand off the wheel to light a cigarette. At one point, when he used one hand for his lighter and the other to shield the flame, it occurred to me that neither one of us would be in shape to radio our "exact location" in the event of an accident.

I breathed a great sigh of relief when we reached our destination—some roughly constructed, cement-floored buildings on a windswept mountain. The mortar platoon had spent the night there and had been busy with weapons drill since early that morning. A shout went up as we rolled to a stop, and I climbed stiffly from the jeep.

"*Casse-croûte pour le Capitaine*," "Snack for the Captain." The procedure was pure Foreign Legion. Within minutes, a trestle table in one of the drafty buildings had been cleared of rucksacks and weapons. The captain indicated a chair for me, and we sat down to a midmorning meal of saucisson, pâté, cheese, crusted bread, red wine, coffee, and a warming jolt of cognac. That done, it was out into the wind again to observe the mortar teams.

The 120mm mortar is a redoubtable weapon. It is heavy both in terms of the destruction it delivers and in terms of its actual weight. Captain Valentin's Legionnaires were manhandling their four weapons over difficult terrain, racing to put them into firing positions, then dismantling them for rapid movement or in preparation for a chopper lift. The mortar's tube weighs 115 kilos, the baseplate 180 kilos, and the two-wheeled cradle 270 kilos. The mortars are usually towed by a small four-wheeled utility vehicle built to be dropped from aircraft. Once near its firing position, the mortar depends on muscle power for its placement.

When the captain left to check with his officers on a nearby firing range, I struck up a conversation with a short British sergeant who had spent twelve years in the Legion. Hands on hips, he was watching his teams erupt from cover in the maquis and spring toward their mortars. Pushing and grunting with effort, the Legionnaires were competing to see which team would be the first ready to fire. The shouting increased. One team seemed to be arguing over the sight setting. The sergeant's face darkened as he waited for the last *chef de pièce* (team leader) to signal his team's readiness with an upraised arm. Once this was done, he shook his head in frustration and motioned for his men to gather round. Addressing them in a voice of quiet disapproval, he told the sweating Legionnaires that there was too much shouting. "Only the *chef de pièce* has that right," he explained. "*Allez*, do it again."

The most efficient team was led by a tall Japanese with a shaved head. He was the first Japanese I had seen during my visit, and I mentioned this to the sergeant.

"They make good soldiers," he told me, his eyes on his men. "We have two types of Japanese in the Legion. The 'samurai' and the 'bureaucrat'. You find the bureaucrats in the offices. That one is a 'samurai'." The platoon was a typical potpourri—men from Portugal, Sweden, Spain, Japan, Croatia, Poland, Moldavia, and Argentina—all working in a tight grouping of teams.

The weighty baseplates bit into the soft earth, and the mortar tubes clanked into place, while elevation and traversing wheels were spun to match the target coordinates. This time only the squad leaders were giving orders. The sergeant nodded his approval.

One deadly technique perfected by the Legion is the "battery flash," a grouping of four or more 120mm mortars firing simultaneously on the same target with devastating effect. Although the Legion is also equipped with the 81mm (Brandt) mortar, the 120mm provides its heavy, in-house fire support.

The Legionnaires run through several additional drills before the captain returns. Then it is time for an alfresco lunch of broiled chicken, noodles, salad, cheese, bread, beer, or wine, followed by strong black coffee. The officers and noncoms eat together at a makeshift table. There is considerable chiding and laughing as the meal is served by Legionnaires on KP. A Pole with less than serviceable French has a hard time understanding a lieutenant who is telling him to reheat the chicken. It becomes a poor-man's version of the British TV sitcom "Fawlty Towers" starring John Cleese. In this case, the officer assumes the role of Mr. Fawlty, with the Pole as the dense Spanish waiter, Manuel.

> *Lieutenant:* "The chicken is cold. Reheat it."
> *Legionnaire:* "Is cooked."
> *Lieutenant:* "I know it's cooked. But take it back for heating."
> *Legionnaire,* putting serving plate back on the table: "Is done. Is cooked."
> *Lieutenant: "Bon Dieu!* Do I have to do it myself?"

Mercifully, a few shouted words from another Pole clarify the situation. The Legionnaire lopes back to the kitchen with the chicken, and the lieutenant swears he will nominate the Pole for an intensive French language course.

Dark thunder clouds were hanging over the mountains when I rode out to a rough firing range where pop-up targets were testing the marksmen of another platoon. A lieutenant was showing his men how to occupy and fire from defensive positions. A thin French *caporal-chef* with the look of a sheepherder— he joined the Legion as a citizen of Monaco—was harrying a squad as they moved through the thick bush toward their firing positions. He was not pleased with his men's dispersal and bombarded those crowding together with pebbles that bounded off their helmets or stung their shoulders.

"*Quoi, Jambon, vous aimez vôtre chef de pièce?*" "What, you ham, in love with your *chef de pièce?*," he shouted at a Legionnaire within two feet of his squad leader. When the squad is finally deployed in an acceptable manner and about to fire, the lieutenant noticed one of the rifles at a strange angle to the target emplacement.

"Watch that one," he shouted to the *caporal-chef,* "he's going to hit the (concrete) firing stand." Within seconds, the *caporal-chef* had straightened the rifle and given the offender's helmet a solid whack. The squad leader shouted to his men, allotting them specific zones to cover with their fire. The lieutenant manipulated the targets electrically. They popped up, and the firing began. Once hit, a target fell, and the riflemen concentrated on another silhouette. One Legionnaire was having trouble with his magazine feed. The *caporal-chef* went forward to assist and remained with the laggard until he completed his firing.

Neither the lieutenant nor the *caporal-chef* was content with his squads' performance. After another glance at the lowering sky, they decided to start once again. The men regrouped and passed in front of us. The Legionnaires were dripping with perspiration. The *caporal-chef* watched them pass and smiled. "*Schwitzen spart Blut,*" he remarked. "Sweat saves blood."

On the way back to Camp Raffalli, the captain stopped to inspect an LZ (landing zone) for a night operation. Naval helicopters were to come in, pick up his mortars, and deposit them in a new position. He eyed the field, the hedges, and the treetops, alert to any power lines. Satisfied, he climbed back into the jeep. The captain had nothing but praise for the pilots of the *Aeronavale* as we turned onto the main road, and the jeep's tires hummed along the asphalt.

"The Navy pilots are always ready to come in at night," he told me, "even when they haven't scouted the LZ in daylight."

It was suddenly flashback time. One of the most solid links of professional camaraderie to emerge from the Indochina War had been that between the paras and the pilots of the *Aeronavale.* Whether pinned down under fire in a Tonkinese rice paddy or slugging it out with a Vietminh regiment in the mountains of northwest Vietnam, the paras knew they could depend on the daredevil naval pilots for support. Roaring in over the muddy delta or swiveling through the jagged limestone mountains in their stubby Bearcats and swept-wing Corsairs, the "flying sailors" delivered lethal air support when it was needed and at great risk. The paras on the ground knew that the Navy pilots, flying from their distant bases in Hanoi or Laos, or from carriers off Haiphong, had a limited amount of time on target. But the airmen often pushed their attacks to the limit, risking empty fuel tanks, before waggling their wings and heading back to base. They say things do not change, but it was indeed strange to hear a new generation Legion parachute officer voluntarily praising the *Aeronavale* more than forty-two years later.

That evening I shared a cous-cous with a full table of officers at the Cercle Sampiero mess. It was plentiful and authentic, complete with spicy merguez sausage, chick peas, and a fiery hot sauce. The cous-cous turned our thoughts to North Africa. I contributed some tales about my two years in revolutionary Algiers operating under a Swiss flag at the American Interests Section. I explained that the former colonial Yacht Club of Algiers, located within the Naval Base, had become a popular luncheon rendezvous for the well-dressed officials of the "revolutionary government" and their Eastern Bloc guests who savored the grilled rouget and steaks washed down with Algerian Rosé much in the manner of the French *fonctionnaires* who preceded them.

Then it was the Legion's turn. There is nothing that seems to inspire a Legionnaire more than the desert. They may no longer be garrisoned in isolated Saharan outposts, and Edith Piaf is no longer singing of the Legionnaire who "smells of warm sand." Nevertheless, with personnel on duty in the Republic of Djibouti, Chad, and the Central African Republic, the Legion's links with the desert are far from severed.

There was talk of mirages, sandstorms, lone tribal snipers, the tyranny of the sun, and the primordial importance of water. More wine encouraged more poetic descriptions. These included the words "mystery," "majesty," and praise for the desert's "great silence." Much of the discussion centered on the desert regions of Chad where the regiment assumed its first real operational role following the Algerian War.

4

—ֺ◈ֺ—

RETURN TO THE DESERT

> The worst of the desert was sandburn. During a sandstorm, the lashing grains work like sandpaper on exposed flesh and produce bleeding.
>
> Retired Legionnaire speaking of the 1969 campaign in Chad

The patrol of fast-moving vehicles, seen from the air, resembled landbound speedboats, as they threw thick plumes of dun-colored dust in their wakes. If an aerial observer had dipped lower for a closer look at the convoy, he would have seen heavily armed men with their heads wrapped in the turban-like folds of the Saharan *cheche*, their faces brown from caked dust, their eyes protected by tinted sand goggles. They resembled an Arab raiding party, or a band of smugglers heading for their mountain hideout; yet, these were Legionnaires. The 2nd REP had returned to Africa—and the desert—in April 1969.

The comparatively rapid decolonization of French territories in Africa during the early 1960s and the defense and economic links maintained with these former colonies had hastened the formation of a viable French Rapid Reaction Force. The commander of the ground force component of this new organization was the general commanding the 11th Parachute Division. Thus, the 2nd REP—as a member of the division—was on call, if needed, as was the 1st REC (*Régiment Étranger de Cavalerie*), the Legion's Cavalry (Armored) Regiment.

Each parachute regiment in the division was instructed to maintain a *Guépard* (Cheetah) detachment ready to depart within six hours of receiving an alert notice. These 390-man contingents were divided into a headquarters element, two combat companies, an 81mm mortar platoon, and a command and service company. If required, this basic detachment could be reinforced rapidly. The written plans for such deployments are always produced with great attention to detail and timing but the gods of war and particularly the demigods of "limited intensity conflict" make their own rules.

Major de Chastenet, the commander of the 2nd REP's *Guépard* detachment had been warned on April 15, 1969, that his unit would be leaving for Chad within a month's time. Within hours, that order had been countermanded. A telegram from Chad had arrived at the ministry of defense reporting that a unit of the French-trained Chadian Army had fallen into a rebel ambush with the loss of all its armament. This was not the first time such a disaster had occurred, and it served to alert the Elysée Palace to the true gravity of the situation. Major de Chastenet's plans for a leisurely preparation went out the window when he was informed that the departure of his *Guépard* detachment was set for that evening.

Long before this attack, President Tombalbaye of Chad had addressed a personal plea for help to General deGaulle. Over one hundred military advisers had been sent to reinforce the Chadian Army. Despite this move, the situation had disintegrated. The revolt had spread, and the Soviet Union, as well as the revolutionary regimes in both Libya and the Sudan, had taken a special supportive interest in the Chadian rebels.

The antigovernment unrest in Chad, which had begun in 1965 with demonstrations against tax collectors and the local *gendarmerie*, had escalated by 1969 into an armed rebellion of tribes and war lords under the banner of the FROLINAT (*Front de Libération National du Chad*). The revolt, however, had roots far deeper than the post-World War II struggles for national liberation. It was fired by tribalism, racialism, religious differences, and ancient animosities. For centuries, the nomadic Islamic Arabs of the arid northern deserts had dominated the black tribes of the more fertile south, raiding their villages and taking slaves.

With independence, the majority black population, including many mission-educated Christians, had taken over the important government posts. Pressures from this new, independent government and the siren song of Muslim brotherhood from Libya and the Sudan had rallied much of the northern populace to the cause of FROLINAT.

The Chad assignment found the Legion in Central Africa for the first time. Like their predecessors in past campaigns, the Legionnaires were adapting quickly to their new environment. This was owing in large part to Major de Chastenet, the commander of Tactical Headquarters No. 1, the *Guépard* unit from the 2nd REP. He had spent two years in the Sahara and knew the deceptive power of the desert sun and its hazards. He insisted that his men be issued wide-brimmed bush hats, sand goggles, and *cheches*.

A retired squad leader at the Legion retirement home at Puyloubier recalled those early days in Chad.

"Strict discipline," he said, "was essential to survival in a desert where the heat reached debilitating temperatures even in the shade." He spoke of three basic rules—respect for basic hygiene, no alcohol, and close control of water consumption.

The Chad veteran emphasized how important it was for his men to keep covered "like the Arabs" to avoid sunburn "that can inflict second degree burns" and sunstroke. He had seen to it that newly arrived Legionnaires did not wear shorts nor roll up their sleeves. He taught them how to use the *cheche* scarf to cover their heads and necks and gave them sandals to wear in place of their boots. "I told them to watch the Arabs, to wear more clothes rather than less but to make sure they were loose and light."

Major de Chastenet's contingent was in Chad to maintain a French *présence*, a matter of showing the tricolor while supporting the wavering Chadian Army. The Legion was not to use its weapons unless fired upon, and there was always the hope that its mere presence might dampen the military ardor of the rebels. These sinewy northerners were hard men, though, survivors in a harsh, dry territory where personal disputes or arguments over rights to water wells were often settled with razor sharp *sagaies*—the tulip-bladed throwing spears of the region—or with the flat report of an aged but well-cared-for Mauser rifle.

At dawn on April 28, 1969, after a brief period of acclimatization and organization, Major de Chastenet led his Legionnaires out of Fort Lamy (now N'Djamena) on their first mission. Their aged vehicles, drawn from the Fort Lamy motor pool, had seen better days. Their objective was the town of Mongo, where an advance base was to be established, and the village of Malgalmé in Guera Province, a region known for rebel activities. On reaching Mongo, de Chastenet split his command, sending his 2nd Company under Captain Milin to the north, while he took the southern route with the 1st Company.

It was not long before Captain Milin spotted an ominous manifestation of rebel presence. A section of the road had been made impassable by a series of cuts dug into the surface in a piano key pattern. Milin and his officers recognized this as the same technique used by the FLN in Algeria and the Vietminh in Indochina. It was a classic guerrilla tactic designed to slow a convoy and make it vulnerable to ambush.

The ambush was not long in coming, and it was like nothing the Legionnaires had faced previously. A shouting, gesticulating mob of 300 rebels armed with *sagaies, coupe-coupes,* and rifles had suddenly appeared on a nearby hill and charged toward the center of the convoy in an attempt to isolate a small detachment of paras. Former Legion officer and writer Pierre Sergent described the reactions of Lieutenant Chiaroni in his book "*2ème REP*." Completely isolated, the lieutenant, working the radio in his jeep put out a call for help to "everyone." "I'm going to have my balls cut off," he announced, "if you don't come *tout de suite*." The lieutenant and two other Legionnaires, armed only with pistols, then hid among the nearby rocks. The rebels vented their fury on the abandoned jeep, firing into the seat cushions and spearing holes in the gas tank.

Aware that more vehicles would soon blunder into the ambush, Lieutenant Chiaroni sent his *adjudant-chef* scuttling among the rocks to warn them off. It was a timely move that stopped a tanker truck and a repair vehicle and saved their drivers from certain death. Fortunately, one of the drivers, a sergeant, was among the best marksmen in the regiment. Within seconds, he had calmly assumed a kneeling position, and a rebel was falling at each crack of his weapon. The rebels' frenzy around the captured jeep abated when they became fully aware of their losses. The 2nd Platoon then arrived as a relieving force, and its machine gun was soon in position and firing. The ambushers fled for the hills, taking the jeep's radio with them.

"That ambush was well prepared," Major de Chastenet wrote later. "Several armed groups positioned to stop the vehicles, two assault groups, or 150–200 men, armed with *sagaies* and cadred by ten or more with firearms . . . a leader commanding from a distance with a whistle. Something very curious, and that I can hardly believe, during the entire ambush, a radio net on our frequency was sending orders in Russian that coincided perfectly with the rebels' maneuvers."

This first contact with the rebels in Chad had cost the 2nd REP two vehicles and a radio. The rebels—who had thought they were attacking a Chadian Army convoy because of the Legionnaires' *cheches* and Saharan dress—had lost fifty dead.

The rainy season during May 1969 turned the roads and trails into mud runs with the consistency of molasses. They were impassable for normal vehicles to say nothing of the reconstituted museum pieces available to the 2nd REP. Lt. Colonel de Chastenet decided to leave a platoon of the 1st Company at Mangalmé while the rest of his command established itself at Mongo. With the trucks sidelined and helicopters hard to come by, the colonel ordered Lieutenant Pietri, the platoon commander, to form his men into a mounted unit. Thirty-five horses were eventually purchased at a market in Mongo. Some had never been ridden before and had to be broken by a Legion corporal, a former jockey, before being sent on to Lieutenant Pietri. History repeated itself as the new "mounted platoon" followed in the hoofprints of the Legion's *Compagnies Montées,* mule-mounted units that patrolled the Moroccan-Algerian frontier during the early 1900s. Pietri's mounted paras maintained a mobility denied to most mechanized units during the tropical rains.

By 1970 the 2nd REP was involved in operations against rebel forces in the rugged Tibesti mountain region of northwest Chad. This was the domain of the Toubou tribe, a redoubtable race of hardened warriors. On March 1, the 1st Company supported by a detachment of the Chadian *gardes nomades* was pursuing a large rebel band in the Safay region. Contact was made, the fighting became intense, and the commander of the Chadian unit was fatally wounded. At that point, a twenty-seven-year-old doctor serving with the 2nd REP, Captain de Larre de la Dorie, left cover under heavy fire to treat the wounded man. He, in turn, was hit and died shortly thereafter. This was neither the first—nor last—time the Legionnaires would be exposed to Toubou marksmanship.

In October of that year, the 2nd REP's Support and Reconnaissance Company, under Captain Wabinski, fought a thirty-six-hour battle with the Toubous who were occupying positions around the LeClerc Gorge in the Zouar sector. The action cost the company one dead and seven wounded. The Legionnaires accounted for twenty-nine enemy dead. Major Malaterre, the senior officer commanding, described the enemy as "particularly tough and obstinate, excellent, even remarkable, marksmen, using natural cover." In November, two more Legionnaires were killed and twelve were wounded during a similar operation near Fada where the enemy left fifty dead on the ground. By December 20, 1970, the threat had subsided, and the men of the 2nd REP returned to Corsica.

In March 1978, operation *Tacaud 4* brought seven officers, and fifteen noncoms of the 2nd REP back to Chad. Col. Mu'ammar Gadhafi's agents and army were applying pressure along the northern frontier and supporting Goukouni Oueddei, the rebel leader of a "National Unity" group. The small, crack contingent of Legion paras, under Lt. Colonel Lhopitallier, the regiment's second in command, was there to improve the Chadian Army's training. Their orders also permitted them to fight, if the Chadians came under attack and, particularly, to assist in the defense of N'Djamena and its airport.

The rebels were no longer relying solely on *sagaies* and outdated firearms. The Libyans had seen to that. AK-47s, 120 and 81mm mortars, rocket launchers, modern machine guns and two-barreled, rapid-firing antiaircraft guns were now part of their armory.

Within weeks the FAT (*Force Armée Tchadienne*) and the Legionnaires had been in action supported by Jaguar fighters, Puma Pirate Gunships, H34 transport choppers, and Alouette command and observation *helicos*. The battle of Ati on May 19, involving the use of artillery and modern weapons by the enemy, was the group's heaviest engagement. In two days of combat, the task force of Chadians, troops of the 3rd Regiment of Marine Infantry, and Legionnaires under the command of Lt. Colonel Lhopitallier, supported by armor, had recaptured the town of Ati and inflicted heavy losses on the enemy.

On the same day that the Legionnaires of Operation *Tacaud 4* were fighting in the bullet-scarred streets of Ati, the rest of the regiment under the command of Colonel Erulin was jumping into Kolwezi, Zaire. Their task was to rescue its European and African population from massacre at the hands of the "Tigers" of the Congolese National Liberation Front (FLNC). This story will be told in chapter 5.

If the continued active service in Chad had renewed the Legion's links with the desert, it had also introduced new tactics. These were not the result of some esoteric staff study. They were born of necessity, but there were links with the past. The cavaliers of the 1st Cavalry Regiment; the mule-mounted *Compagnies Montées;* and the camel-mounted *Méhariste* units of the Sahara had all been designed to improve mobility on the broad expanses of French-controlled territory in North Africa and the Middle East.

Now, faced with the same problems in Chad, the Legion dusted off the principle of *nomadisation;* the use of fast-moving, long-distance combat patrols, to keep the enemy off balance and to restore confidence to a worried population. Equipped with the latest antitank weapons, mortars, and heavy machine guns, the patrols could profit from deadly force in addition to the element of surprise. The gradually increased use of reconnaissance aircraft, fighters, gunships, and troop-lifting *helicos* gave the ground units eyes, ears, mobility, and added punch.

These *nomadisation* sorties often involved swift movement over hundreds of kilometers of desert terrain that took the paras into rebel-dominated territory. In addition to breaking up enemy formations, the unexpected presence of these Franco-Chadian patrols made the Libyan advisers aware of the increased dangers they were risking in Chad.

The litany of operations continued. In 1983–1984, with N'Djamena directly threatened by the Libyans, operations christened *Manta* (Devilfish) and *Manta-Echo* were launched. For six months during 1984, Colonel Janvier, the regimental commander, and the 1,026 Legionnaires of *Manta-Echo* reestablished peace and order over a wide zone of operations in Eastern Chad, including the return of normal economic activity in the towns of Biltine, Arada, and Iriba. A whole series of operation *Épervier* (Sparrowhawk), from early 1986 to 1994, saw various companies of the 2nd REP come and go. They occupied ancient forts at Abéché and Biltine and scoured the countryside in search of rebel forces. Photos of Legionnaires in white képis standing guard outside the mud-brick walls could have been photos from the early 1900s.

The regiment's *Commandos de Recherche et d'Action dans le Profondeur* (CRAP), its reconnaissance and intelligence team, often joined the companies for special tasks during the Chad operations. Sergeant Mazars of CRAP joined the Legion in 1983 after completing his compulsory military service in the *Gendarmerie.* He has served in Djibouti, Chad, Central Africa, and the Gulf. His team included Legionnaires from Britain, Portugal, Spain, and Germany. He jumped into Chad on a special mission to recover a pilot's body and sensitive material from the wreck of a Jaguar fighter-bomber shot down by the Libyans. The team stayed on to stop Libyan-supported rebel infiltration. Mazars remembers the desert as long flat stretches of rock and dust broken by jagged mountains. The heat made life difficult, but he found sandstorms the principal problem.

"They blocked out the sun, restricted our movements and made both air and land reconnaissance almost impossible." During the storms, the paras wrapped their *cheches* around their heads and sought shelter in their vehicles.

Contacts with the enemy were rare. Various reconnaissance missions revealed the tracks of rebel vehicles in the sand and the bones of the dead in ragged uniforms. At one point, Sergeant Mazars came upon a skeleton with an unexploded rocket-propelled grenade (RPG-7) protruding from its rib cage. When on patrol for fifteen or twenty days, his team routinely augmented its rations with gazelle or guinea hen, thanks to a Chadian officer who acted as a guide to the best hunting grounds.

Lt. Colonel Hogard, the Legion's recruiting officer, served in Chad with the 2nd REP. He has spent more time in Africa than at Camp Raffalli. He recalls northern Chad as a tough operational zone. "The north," he explained, "was much rougher on the men than the south where things were tropical and water was available. Our patrols in the north had to cover 400 kilometers using a compass for navigation."

In 1986 the increased threat of direct Libyan involvement—including artillery and armor—brought a substantial component of French airpower to the Chad theater. Mirage and Jaguar fighters, KC-135 in-flight refuelers, observation aircraft, and Hawk and Crotale suface-to-air missile batteries were deployed. While the paras' prime mission was the protection of N'Djamena and its airfield, there was little doubt they were also there as combat troops and the Chadian leader Hissene Habre's successes against the rebels in May and June of 1987 owed a great deal to the support received from the Legion. The diplomatic dispute over Libyan troop presence in Chad was clarified in 1990, when Colonel Gadhafi authorized the flight to Chad of heavy jet transports to repatriate Libyan prisoners captured during earlier actions.

The irony of this repatriation was that it took place as Idriss Deby, a former chief of staff of the Chadian Army largely responsible for the previous victory over the rebels, was leading his own rebel force toward N'Djamena to overthrow the government of Hissene Habre. Thus, as the paras of the 2nd REP were busy providing security and evacuating 1,600 civilians of all nationalities from the city, they also had to supervise the departure of the Libyan POWs.

By 1994, the Regiment had returned to Chad eleven times. The operational visits were prompted by continuous rebellions, Libyan incursions and subversion, general instability, and threats to French interests and citizens. Considering the continued instability in this desert region, the odyssey of the 2nd REP in Chad is far from finished.

How can the paras of the 2nd REP undertake an operational move within six hours? How can they be ready for the shimmering heat of the Chadian desert, the green hell of some tropical jungle, or the snow drifts of a high altitude mountain pass? Part of the answer lies in preparation. Combat readiness is almost a religion in the Legion. The regiment's supply warehouses at Camp Raffalli contain clothing and equipment to fit jungle-desert-mountain environments and ensure no delays in *Guépard* deployment.

Each Legionnaire in the regiment has his own clothing and equipment stored in a field pack, according to size, and marked with his name, rank, serial number and company designation. For example, the hot weather (desert) pack contains: light clothing, shirts, trousers, shorts, and so forth, two of each item; along with bush boots, light duvet, shelter half, *cheche*, mosquito nets for head and bed, pneumatic mattress, sand goggles with varicolored lenses, dark glasses, and a wide-brimmed bush hat. The para is allowed to change or renew his clothing every six or eight months. The same goes for the mess kit, or *gamelle*, and the one and one-half liter canteen. Provision is made to provide two or three canteens for service in Africa.

The noncom in charge of supplies explained how the 2nd REP's recent experience in Sarajevo had underlined the importance of maintaining a ready stock of cold weather gear. This includes heavy boots, polar fur, and Gortex windbreakers. He emphasized the importance of quality boots. Despite the regiment's delivery to an operational zone by parachute or chopper, the paras still cover many kilometers on foot. Any purchase of boots must be considered carefully in light of the quality-wear-price ratio. The comparative largesse of today's Legion in equipping its men for overseas duty causes some headshaking among veterans.

"It was much harder in the old days," I was told by an *ancien* of the 2nd REP. "Every evening when we returned from a march, the sergeant would ask us to show him the soles of our boots. If any boot nails were missing, we'd have to pay for them ourselves."

Chad and Zaire were not the only territories where the 2nd REP has recently been active in Africa. Since 1973, companies of the regiment had been joining the 13th demibrigade of the Legion in French Djibouti (*Territoire des Afars et des Issas*) on the horn of Africa. Djibouti was—and is—hard duty. The sun burns like an arc light in a pale blue sky, the rocky dry plains stretch to infinity, parts of the city look like a rejected set from some old Bogart classic, and a visit to the camel market just about covers the tourist attractions.

Porous frontiers with Ethiopia and Somalia are the targets of political agents and professional smugglers, banditry is endemic, and a man traveling without a weapon is considered suicidal. The flow of refugees from Ethiopia, depending on the politico-economic state of that nation, is a constant problem. The tanned Legionnaires stationed in Djibouti have always seen it as the place to save pay and allowances, an opportunity to put away a nest-egg for their return to more hospitable climes.

Long, dehydrating border patrols enlivened by the occasional search of a camel caravan and interminable chases of reported infiltrators can grate on the nerves. *Nomadisation* is also the name of the game in Djibouti, and becoming desert-wise is a requirement.

One officer described a tense moment in Djibouti defused by a bit of judicious preplanning. The scout vehicle of his small patrol reported the approach of a large, heavily armed band of Somalis. Placing his sniper with his scoped FR-FI 7.26mm rifle in a concealed firing position, the officer crested the dunes to block the Somali's progress. After some moments of hesitation and palaver, the Somalis began to make threatening gestures and inch toward the Legionnaires. By this time the officer had identified the band's leader. His prearranged signal was followed by the report of the sniper's rifle and a small geyser of sand erupted at the Somali leader's sandaled feet. The macho protocol of the desert had been satisfied. Convinced they were facing a determined man and unsure that the Legion might call in some form of support, the Somalis made a show of turning back toward the border.

During the mid-1970s, the Horn of Africa was the scene of dangerous political and military pressures. The cold war was fully present in a hot climate. The Soviets had established bases to the south of Djibouti—in Mogadishu and Berbera. Across the strategic strait of Bab-el-Mandeb in South Yemen, Cuban and Soviet military advisers were active, and Soviet-backed Somalia was claiming Djibouti as its own.

Early on the morning of February 3, 1976, with independence a little more than a year away, the political antagonisms of the region resulted in high human drama. Seven pro-Soviet Issa gunmen seized a school bus carrying thirty young French children from military families and headed for the Somali frontier. An ultimatum from the terrorist leader demanded:

• Total and immediate independence
• The liberation of all Issa political prisoners
• The return of all arms seized from their members
• The departure of all French military and security forces.

If these demands were not met, "in a short time" the children would be executed.

A Puma helicopter managed to intercept the bus at the palm grove of Loy-

ada and forced it to stop. By noon the bus had inched toward the Somali
frontier post. During the early afternoon, while the French High Commis-
sioner was attempting to negotiate with the terrorists, the 2nd Company of
the 2nd REP, under the command of Captain Soubirou, moved into assault
positions near the vehicle.

The situation was a nightmare. A bus filled with frightened, thirsty children
and seven determined terrorists of the FLCS (*le Front de Libération de la Côte des
Somalis*) armed with automatic weapons and willing to become martyrs. The
seriousness and scope of this crisis called for quick decisions and rapid action.
French officials on the spot, both military and civilian, expected the Somali
border guards to support the kidnappers in the event of a shoot-out. This possibility and an adequate response had to be part of any rescue plan.

Nine expert marksmen from the elite GIGN, (*Groupement d'Intervention de la
Gendarmerie Nationale*, the intervention group of the National Gendarmerie,
were flown in from Paris. Armored cars from the 13th Demi-brigade arrived
to support the paras of the 2nd REP. The planners were faced with two basic
realities—the terrorist demands could not be met, and the children would
have to be rescued with the least possible risk.

The GIGN marksmen were the key to any rescue plan. They were given
the almost impossible task of dropping each of the terrorists with a coordi-
nated, simultaneous fire after a careful countdown. This tactic would call for
constant observation of terrorist movements in and around the bus and close
radio liaison between the marksmen and their commander, Lieutenant Pro-
teau. The paras would rush forward to assault the bus as the first shots were
fired. The armored vehicles of the DBLE and Legionnaires posted on a
nearby roof would be ready to suppress any fire from the Somali side of the
border.

Mademoiselle Jehanne Bru, the director of the children's primary school,
had volunteered to join the young hostages on the bus. Her presence reassured
the children, and she established some order among them, supervising the
distribution of food, water, and blankets supplied by the French authorities. A
restless night and the constant threat of a massacre was forcing a decision. The
situation had not improved by morning; negotiations had reached an impasse.

As most of the children dozed through the siesta period, the GIGN marksmen opened fire, and the 2nd Company of the 2nd REP attacked. One platoon invested a Somali machine gun emplacement and knocked it out. Another platoon sprinted toward the bus in a race against time. The armored
cars of the DBLE rolled forward to deliver covering fire.

Two terrorists had been killed and one had been badly wounded by the
marksmen, but the survivors were preparing to kill the children, when the
Legionnaires leapt into the bus. One terrorist, holding an already wounded
young boy as a shield, was killed with a shot to the head. Another was dropped

with a burst of submachine gunfire as he lifted his weapon. The battle continued around the Somalian border post as Mlle. Bru and her wards were led off
the bus and rushed to the hospital. It was all over in an hour.

Seven terrorists had died, and twenty Somalis were either dead or
wounded. Lieutenant Doucet of the 2nd REP had been seriously wounded,
while leading an assault on the Somali machine-gun position. The casualties
among the children caused particular heartache. Nadine Durand had been
shot to death by a terrorist while being held on the bus driver's lap, and Valerie
Geissbuhler had been fatally wounded in the fusillade. Five other children had
been wounded as had the busdriver and Jehanne Bru. Both Doucet and Bru
would later receive the Legion of Honor for their part in the rescue operation.

Such counterterrorist action is always a difficult task. When children are
involved as hostages, the difficulties are compounded. Once the decisions had
been made at Loyada, everyone involved knew that the success of the mission
depended upon luck and speed. Luck failed when it came to the visibility of
terrorist targets and the ability to knock them all out at the same time. The
speed with which the Legionnaires assaulted the bus could not be faulted. The
2nd REP must be prepared for this type of action, but it is not the sort of operation the paras prefer. One officer summed it up with a few words and a
grimace. "A sad affair," he commented.

When Djibouti became independent in June 1977, the new government
asked the Legion garrison to stay under the terms of a defense agreement
with France. The 13th Demi Brigade remained at Gabode, and the 2nd REP
established a post at Arta. Since then, revolving companies of the 2nd REP
have succeeded each other in Djibouti on tours of duty lasting seventeen to
eighteen weeks. The paras, working in tandem with the 13th DBLE, have
conducted desert training, live-fire exercises, extensive patrols, and searched
for border infiltrators during periods of unrest in neighboring Ethiopia. The
2nd REP's Djibouti assignments ended in May 1994 when the paras left the
sun-baked African republic and their comrades of the 13th DBLE to return
to Camp Raffalli.

Whether or not the regiment has left Djibouti forever, one thing is certain.
It left part of itself in the new republic. On February 3, 1982, during a training
exercise in bad weather, a transport aircraft carrying the 2nd Platoon of the
4th Company smashed into the slopes of Mount Garbi. Captain Philipponat,
second in command of the company, First Sergeant Storai, and twenty-five
noncoms and Legionnaires died in the crash. Members of the 2nd REP and
the 13th DBLE climb Mount Garbi each year to lay a wreath in memory of
their comrades at the simple monument commemorating the tragedy.

While many paras consider themselves experts on desert operations, a number
of them have also passed through the Jungle Commando School in French

Guiana. This overseas department of France is described in the 1993–1994 CIA World Factbook with disconcerting frankness as "mostly an unsettled wilderness." The center, officially designated the *Centre d'Entrainement Forêt Equatorial* (CEFE), is reached by motorized pirogue and is located in the heart of the tropical forest. The Foreign Legion's 3rd Infantry Regiment has been based permanently in French Guiana since 1973, charged with protecting the French Space Center at Kourou, surveillance of the borders with Surinam and Brazil and supervising the CEFE. U.S. Marines, Army Rangers, the British SAS, Canadian and Brazilian Special Forces, troops from the Surinam Defense Forces, and third-year students from the French military academy of St. Cyr have all passed through the CEFE.

Adjudant Etievant has been in the 2nd REP for thirteen years, including seven as a *chuteur opérationnel* with a CRAP Team. Trained as a sniper, a medic, and an expert in hand-to-hand combat, he was assigned to the 3rd Infantry Regiment and sent to the CEFE in 1992. At that time, the regiment's commander, Colonel Serveille, was the only *chef du corps* who had passed through the Brazilian Commando School, "the toughest in the world both physically and mentally," according to Etievant.

On arriving at Regina for his two-year assignment, Etievant was initiated into life in the jungle with the minimal survival techniques—how to make a fire without matches, to wash without fail morning and night, and to live with the oppressive heat. These requirements may sound simple, but they are essential to operating effectively in the jungle. One month later, he traveled by motorized pirogue to the *Centre d'Entrainement Forêt Equatorial* (CEFE) instruction zone, located on a small mountain six kilometers from the center.

When I spoke with Etievant at Camp Raffalli, he was still lean and tanned from his stint in the jungle. He briefed me with considerable enthusiasm on the rules for jungle survival:

- Always have a rifle, magazines, and ammunition with you wherever you go, for any reason.
- You will be punished if you disobey this rule.
- Never leave camp alone. If you must leave, inform a sentry of your planned absence.
- If you become lost, avoid panic. Halt and fire three shots. Wait five minutes and fire three more. Repeat procedure several times.
- If this fails to bring help, find a stream of any size and follow it to a river. All rivers in French Guiana flow to the sea, and villages are to be found on the river banks. Remember, "the river is life."
- Eat and drink all that can be taken from the jungle plants and foliage. Use banana leaves to form a pot for boiling water. Most jungle wood is waterlogged, but white-trunked trees will burn. Learn to identify the "milk tree." Its pulp and sap are full of vitamins and minerals.

- Test all jungle fruit before eating. Rub some on your inner forearm and wait for reaction. If redness appears, throw away the fruit. Or, put your tongue on fruit briefly. If your tongue reddens, swells, or burns, do not eat the fruit. If you are desperate, test fruit by eating a small piece slowly every fifteen minutes. Always be cautious. Watch animals, particularly monkeys, to see if they eat fruit without dire results.

During a special three-day survival test, each man is briefed on jungle plants and given a fishing line, hooks, a rifle, fifteen rounds of ammunition, one machete, and three matches. They are searched to ensure that they are not carrying rations or extra supplies. Legionnaires learn to eat the raw meat of snared or shot animals, earthworms, and the white grubs found in decaying tree trunks. They use the juice from a select forest liana that, released into a stream, paralyzes or kills fish and crabs. Some Legionnaires have become adept at tree climbing in search of bird eggs.

The *adjudant* had little patience with those who had problems finding food during their three-day survival test. He was particularly unimpressed with some of the American participants.

"U.S. troops always had fall-back rations on hand," he explained. "They tended to give up the search for food and fishing to go to sleep. They felt too secure and knew they could slow down."

Etievant summed up his jungle experience in one sentence. "Everything is easy, if a man's morale, his mental state, is good."

The regimental insignia of the Foreign Legion's 2ème Régiment Étranger de Parachutistes (2nd REP) incorporates the burning grenade symbol of the Foreign Legion and the dragon of Annam, which commemorates the regiment's first active duty (as a battalion) during the First Indochina War. *BIHLE/Aubagne**

The winged dagger emblem, worn by members of all French parachute units. *BIHLE/Aubagne.*

*All Foreign Legion photographs were provided courtesy of the Bureau d'Information et Historique de la Légion Étrangère in Aubagne (the Office of Information and History, French Foreign Legion Headquarters, Aubagne, France, or BIHLE/Aubagne).

A noncommissioned officer inspects the guard detachment at Camp Raffalli. *BIHLE/Aubagne.*

The 2nd REP on parade at their headquarters at Camp Raffalli on the Mediterranean island of Corsica. *BIHLE/Aubagne.*

The men of the 2nd REP's 1st Company specialize in antitank warfare and night fighting. Here they practice house-to-house combat on a range near Camp Raffalli. *BIHLE/Aubagne.*

Paras of the 1st Company perfect their fighting techniques under highly realistic conditions. *BIHLE/Aubagne.*

The 2nd Company, which specializes in mountain warfare, prepares for Alpine operations. *BIHLE/Aubagne.*

A para of the 2nd Company undergoing mountain training in the Alps. The Legionnaires find that light, sound, and distance, in a high-altitude setting, can play tricks on their senses. *BIHLE/Aubagne.*

The paras of the 2nd Company must be as adept at cross-country skiing as they are at mountain climbing. *BIHLE/Aubagne.*

Second Company alpinists climbing in the rugged Corsican mountains. *BIHLE/Aubagne.*

The 2nd Company during an Alpine operation. *BIHLE/Aubagne.*

The 2nd Company practices house-to-house combat outside its preferred element. *BIHLE/Aubagne.*

A French Navy submarine keeps its rendezvous with paras of the 3rd Company in the Bay of Calvi. Paras of the 3rd Company are experts on amphibious operations, underwater infiltration, and combat swimming. *BIHLE/Aubagne.*

Combat swimmers from the 3rd Company jump from a French Navy Super-Frelon helicopter in the Bay of Calvi. *BIHLE/Aubagne.*

A combat swimmer of the 3rd Company is hauled aboard a Zodiac inflatable boat after parachuting into the Bay of Calvi. *BIHLE/Aubagne.*

Paras of the 3rd Company secure their Zodiac to the deck of a submarine. *BIHLE/Aubagne.*

Combat swimmers rush ashore with their equipment. *BIHLE/Aubagne.*

Beach assault by specialists of the 3rd Company. *BIHLE/Aubagne.*

High in the Corsican mountains, a chopper picks up paras of the 3rd Company. *BIHLE/Aubagne.*

An instructor keeps his binoculars on the target as members of the 3rd Company complete their qualification with the Minimi light machine gun.

Photo by the author.

A para of the 4th Company ready for action. His unit specializes in mine warfare and sniping. *BIHLE/Aubagne.*

Demolition experts of the 4th Company simulate blowing up a bridge during a training exercise. *BIHLE/Aubagne.*

A mortar team of the 4th Company in action. *BIHLE/Aubagne.*

The 2nd REP's CEA (Compagnie d'Éclairage et d'Appui), the company responsible for reconnaissance and fire support, keeps things rolling during patrol near their base in Djibouti. *BIHLE/Aubagne.*

The rapid-firing 20mm cannon of the 2nd REP's CEA in action during a training exercise. *BIHLE / Aubagne.*

5

---=◈◈◈=---

INTO THE UNKNOWN

It was my first action but not what I expected. There was some ground fire. Five meters from the Drop Zone, I came upon a small pile of severed human hands.

> Lt. Col. Bon recalling his jump as a young Lieutenant at Kolwezi, Zaire, at 1640 hours on May 19, 1978.

Lieutenant Bon made his macabre discovery after hitting the ground near Kolwezi, an important copper mining center in Zaire's Shaba (formerly Katanga) Province. He had come face to face with the strange world of African witchcraft for the first time. Bon was one of the 400 legionnaires of the 2nd REP dropped into the high elephant grass with the first assault wave on the afternoon of May 19, 1978, by a small force of five Zairian Hercules C-130s and two French Air Force Transall C-160s. Their heavy equipment was being flown to the closest large airfield at Lubumbashi by eight U.S. Air Force C-141 Starlifters and a C-5A Galaxy, provided through an agreement with the Carter White House.

The operation was baptized *Bonite* (Bonito). The regiment was commanded by Colonel Philippe Erulin, a tough, stolid parachute officer and veteran of the Algerian conflict. Its mission—to rescue twenty-five hundred Europeans and many more Zairians threatened with massacre by the "Tigers" of the *Front de Libération Nationale Congolais* (FLNC) and end the rebel threat to the town and the surrounding area.

A task force of Belgian paracommandos was being organized by the Brussels government, but foot-dragging and political argument had delayed their arrival in the former Belgian colony. With hundreds of French civilian lives at stake, and members of the French military mission to Zaire already reported missing and probably in rebel hands, Paris had decided to act on its own. A direct appeal for assistance to President Giscard d'Estaing by President Mobutu Sese Seko Waza Banga had hardened the French resolve.

The cold war was a reality in 1978. Africa had been divided haphazardly into spheres of influence between the opposing superpowers. Intelligence agents of all hues were thick on the ground, international mercenaries had not yet faded from the scene, clandestine arms shipments were commonplace, and the East-West struggle often turned violent with the profuse spilling of blood, most of it African. Zaire's strategic position and its mineral wealth in commercial diamonds, copper, colombite, cobalt, zinc, uranium, and pewter made it a particular prize. Shaba Province, the region under attack, was the richest in natural resources. Soviet, Cuban, East German, and Czech military advisers and "spooks" based in Angola supplied the "Katangais" with equipment and expertise. The French, Americans, Chinese and Belgians had rallied to President Mobuto's side.

This was not the first time the FLNC had attempted to invade what they still called "Katanga." A year earlier, Moroccan units, flown to Zaire by French military aircraft, had helped the Zairian Army repulse an earlier raid by the "Katangais."

No one had elaborated a "domino theory" for Africa, but Zaire, with its strategic central position and huge francophone population, was seen as a keystone to the survival of a non-Communist Africa. Highly classified messages flashed back and forth between Paris and its civilian and military representatives in Zaire and neighboring African countries. The French High Command was faced with the urgent need to make an important decision. What unit could respond quickly and effectively to such an emergency?

It was not a difficult choice. The 2nd REP was given the nod. One of its detachments was already in Africa helping to block Libya's incursion into Chad, and the 2nd REP's quick reaction capabilities were well known. In addition, unlike some other parachute units of the 11th Parachute Division, it had no conscripts in its ranks. The paras of the 2nd REP were all volunteers. Furthermore, the 2nd REP's island location meant that many Legionnaires hesitated to travel to the mainland on their infrequent leaves. The preparation for movement on short notice was a regimental procedure that had been followed many times, both as an exercise and as the real thing.

The 2nd REP was put on a six-hour *Guépard* (cheetah) alert at 1000 hours on May 17, 1978. This meant that Colonel Erulin's Legionnaires must be equipped and ready to move in six hours' time. Men undergoing special training at Corte and Bonifacio in Corsica and Mont Louis on the mainland were rushed back to Camp Raffalli. A strident siren sounding from the camp called those paras on leave in Calvi back to their base. MP patrols drove through the garrison town to speed the process. By 2000 hours the regiment was ready. At 0500 the next morning, the paras clambered into trucks for the trip to the airport of Solenzara. Four commercial DC-8s and one Boeing 707 were waiting there to load the first group of paras for their long voyage to Kinshasa, the Zairian capital, and a combat operation six thousand kilometers from their base.

American military representatives were invited to attend planning meetings to elaborate details of U.S. assistance in the form of transport aircraft and specific support equipment.

The French action was accelerated on May 18, when Zairian military intelligence intercepted a radio message from Lt. General M'Bumba in Angola addressed to the Tiger commander in Kolwesi, Major Mufu. The message ordered the assassination of foreign hostages, the destruction of several factories, and the forced evacuation of the African population.

This was in stark contrast with *Ordre de Service 01* issued on April 20 by Lt. General M'Bumba and soon to be in the hands of the 2nd REP's intelligence officer. That document listed plans and the do's and dont's for operation *Colombe,* or Dove—the code name for the rebel's Kolwezi campaign. Item No. 4 of this order warned, "It is strictly forbidden to threaten, mistreat, or even touch in any way the foreigners working at the *l'Union Minière du Haut Katanga* as well as in all the other companies of the liberated regions." It also warned commanders to keep their men out of Kolwezi's beer halls and promised severe penalties for rape.

Since May 13, armed groups of the Tigers, former Katangan Gendarmerie exiled in Zambia and Angola, had infiltrated Shaba Province. Led by Lt. Gen. Nathanael M'Bumba, a former police official in the government of Moise Tshombe, the rebels were organized, uniformed, and wore a shoulder patch depicting a charging yellow tiger. They were well armed, well trained, and cadred by Cuban and East German advisers. Early intelligence reports had placed two thousand or more Tigers in Kolwezi. The most recent figures estimated the remaining enemy force at just over 500. These troops were said to be supported by a number of locally recruited irregulars. The most troubling reports from both civilian and military sources told of wholesale massacres and of African and European corpses littering the empty streets of the town.

After an attempt at resistance that cost them dearly, the troops of Zairian President Mobutu's army had fled, leaving behind five Panhard armored cars and quantities of arms and ammunition. The French-trained 311th Parachute Battalion of the Zairian Army under the command of Major Mahele had moved into a defensive position on May 16, securing a bridge thirty-five kilometers west of Kolwezi. One of its companies—dropped near Kolwezi—had taken heavy casualties.

The Legionnaires drifting down toward the Kolwezi DZ in the afternoon heat amid sporadic ground fire were dropping into an unknown situation. About 50 percent of the paras were landing outside the DZ, their antitank weapons (LRAC-89mm) would be hard to retrieve, and tall grass and high ant hills would make regrouping difficult. Six men had already been wounded by enemy automatic weapons fire. The regiment's first fatality, Legionnaire Arnold, a Briton who had gone off in search of his antitank weapon, would be found the next day on the edge of the DZ, dead from a head wound, his body mutilated.

Upon entering the old sector of town, the Legionnaires were immediately involved in bitter house-to-house fighting. The urgent need to rescue the hostages was foremost in their minds. Grimacing at the sight and stench of swollen, unburied corpses, they advanced street by street. Firefights erupted as the Tigers launched sudden counterattacks.

These were not the Congolese "Simba" tribesmen of 1964, facing modern weaponry secure in the knowledge that their amulets, gris-gris, and magic body paint would protect them from harm. These were uniformed troops with an appreciation of the value of firepower. Their heterogeneous armament included Italian submachine guns, Soviet Kalashnikovs, Belgian FAL rifles, Chinese mortars, Soviet antitank grenades, and various rocket launchers and mines. Although shaken and disoriented by the unexpected appearance of the paras, the Tigers were now showing a suprising determination to stand their ground.

At one point, the paras found themselves blocked and under fire from two of the captured Panhard armored cars manned by the rebels. Direct hits from the Legion's antitank weapons destroyed the vehicles, and the surviving crew members fled into the narrow streets.

The regiment's sharpshooters proved particularly effective during the street fighting. They calmly marked their targets, fired their scoped sniper rifles without haste, and dropped the enemy at distances of 300 to 400 meters and beyond. Excerpts from the regiment's *Journal de Marche* give a dispassionate account of the fighting.

> Advancing toward their objectives: a bridge over the northern hook of the lake and railroad bridge, the squads were harassed and fired on constantly. Our sharpshooters killed a number of rebels, but close to the *école technique* the Tiger's resistance hardened.

> Arriving within sight of the railroad bridge, the lead squad (Sergeant Sablek) was taken under fire by a dozen marksmen posted around the *école technique* and the northern outskirts of the Manika quarter. Sergeant Moreau's squad outflanked them to the north, supported by Sablek, and killed ten rebels, capturing seven weapons. At the same time, seven rebels in the *école technique* were put out of action by our sharpshooters.
>
> The 1st Platoon of Lieutenant Bourgain, having cleaned out the *école technique* and neutralized fifteen rebels, continued its action toward the *Gendarmerie* fifty meters to the south . . .

The advancing paras then faced the most difficult part of operation *Bonite*—the search for possible survivors and the rumored charnel houses where General M'Bumba's assassination order had been carried out. A search of the cellars at the bloodstained Hotel Impala revealed twenty swollen, decomposing cadavers. The Legionnaires then accomplished the dramatic liberation of one group of prisoners. Cries in French of "Don't shoot!" were heard by the paras of the 4th Squad when they fought their way to the town's Gendarmerie headquarters still occupied by the Tigers. After killing the five rebel defenders, the paras freed thirty-five hostages—twenty-six whites and nine Africans. The Belgians, French, Americans, and Zairians, some wounded and all filthy from being forced to live in their own excrement, joined in singing a shaky "La Marseillaise" to mark their liberation.

The obscurity of the equatorial night had slammed down like a black fire curtain early on the evening of May 19. With it came a sudden, surprising drop in temperature that cooled the Legionnaires' perspiration and brought on a sudden chill. Lt. Colonel Bon noted that many of the enemy had withdrawn at first sight of the drop aircraft. But enough remained, sniping and mounting fruitless counterattacks, to keep the Legionnaires busy all night. Bright moonlight helped the paras inflict further casualties and prevent the enemy from regrouping. The paras had jumped equipped only for combat and without sleeping sacks or blankets. They wrapped themselves in their parachutes for warmth, and those not in action or on patrol ate their American-supplied rations without great enthusiasm. Bon remembers he could not stomach the peanut butter.

During the night, the paras retook the garages belonging to the principal nationalized mining company, *Gecamines*. This provided the Legionnaires with vehicles and a certain measure of mobility. More hard contacts came with dawn.

"The enemy fired rocket launchers," Bon recalls. "There was a veritable firestorm from automatic weapons and mortars. I directed the fire of our grenade launchers. One of the Legion officers fought a face-to-face pistol duel with a "Tiger" at 15 meters distance—and won. The rebels had been drinking and they were smoking *Kif* (hashish). The company charged and took many prisoners. We soon had so many we had to let most of them go."

In addition to the prisoners, the Legionnaires of Bon's company captured a number of arms including Stens, Mausers, automatic rifles of various makes, Israeli Uzis, and U.S. M-16s.

Recalling his own entry into the silent streets of Kolwezi, Lt. Colonel Bon frowned as he described what he found. "The town was wide open. No one had taken care of the many corpses lying among the houses and in the streets. The town's dogs were gorged with human flesh. My Legionnaires, trying to identify the dead, were faced with an unusual problem. Whites turn black when putrifying, and blacks white."

The second wave of the regiment, delayed the previous evening and its drop canceled, jumped at 0630 on May 20. This added 250 men and an 81mm mortar section to the 400 Legionnaires already on the ground. When the Legionnaires of the 4th Company arrived at the former headquarters of the Zairian Army, they made a stomach-wrenching discovery. The fly-covered corpses of more than forty European hostages filled one of the rooms. Men, women, children, and infants piled on top of one another, ripped by bullets and grenade fragments. A sole female survivor was found hidden under the dead.

On the morning of May 20, a battalion of Belgian paracommandos arrived at Kolwezi airstrip now held by the 311th Zairian Parachute Battalion. Their immediate task was to evacuate the European population, while the 2nd REP continued its mop-up operation in and around Kolwezi.

During a particularly violent battle for the *Metal-Shaba* complex held by 200 rebels, the marksmanship of the Legionnaires paid off once again. French war correspondent Jean François Chauvel described how a twenty-year-old Legionnaire used his high precision, scoped sniper's rifle to kill a rebel machine gunner at 200 meters. When the machine gun began to fire again, he dropped the second gunner. When a Tiger tried to relocate the weapon, he, too, was shot. As Chauvel relates, "There wasn't a fourth attempt." The regiment lost one of its top noncoms, Sergent-Chef Daniel, during this clash. The Tigers left eighty dead behind.

When the vehicles transported to Zaire by the U.S. Air Force arrived from Lubumbashi, the Legionnaires enlarged the scope of their patrols, seeking the enemy wherever he could be found, blocking his escape routes, and searching for more hostages. Some European fugitives, found hiding in the bush without food or water, tearfully told of those not so fortunate who had been abducted when the Tigers evacuated the town. Others spoke of the foreign advisers operating with the rebels, one of whom—an East German—was heard complaining about the Tiger's "disorder and lack of discipline." Traumatized children hesitantly told how they had seen their parents butchered.

Sporadic fighting continued until May 26. By May 27, Colonel Erulin had regrouped his regiment at Lubumbashi and the 2nd REP's mission was completed. On May 28, intelligence reported General M'Bumba's troops recrossing the border into Angola, and an inter-African Force was on its way to replace the Legionnaires.

The abortive invasion had cost the Tigers of the FLNC 250 dead and many more wounded. Two armored cars and numerous jeeps and trucks had been destroyed. A thousand weapons had been captured, including four recoilless rifles, fifteen mortars, twenty-one antitank weapons, ten machine guns, and thirty-eight automatic rifles. One hundred and ninety Europeans had been killed by the rebels; another forty who had been taken hostage were later found murdered. Five hundred and twenty-one Zairian civilians had been massacred. The 2nd REP losses included five Legionnaires killed and twenty wounded. The lives of hundreds of European and African hostages had been spared, and Zaire's Shaba Province had been secured. In the curious context of the overheated cold war struggle for Africa, the West had won a small but significant victory.

On June 7, after a triumphant parade in Lubumbashi attended by President Mobutu, the 2nd REP boarded U.S. Air Force Starlifters for their return flight to Calvi. Shortly after returning to Camp Raffalli, the regiment added another citation "*a l'ordre de l'armée*" to its battle honors. General Lagarde, Chief of Staff of the Army Ground Forces presided over the ceremonies and read the citation that began with the words "Magnificent Regiment that, since its creation in 1948, has not ceased to distinguish itself in the service of France. . . ."

Perhaps the most impressive, if unusual, praise for the 2nd REP's action at Kolwezi came in the form of an anonymous letter from a militant of the French Communist Party addressed to Colonel Erulin.

> I am not in the habit of writing to express my admiration or approbation. In fact, I never do. I am a *convinced communist* (sic) with responsibilities within the CGT [*Confédération Générale de Travail*—communist dominated labor union].
>
> I must tell you of my complete opposition to the allegations of our federal leaders. In France, naturally, one hundred percent of the right is with you. But you should know that—among us communists—ninety nine percent agree with operation *Guépard* at Kolwezi. Following a discussion of our cell, not one of us was against the operation. You should know that—on the word of a communist.

The only image we retain in the middle of all that drama is the mother, holding her child in her arms, and watching "*les pepins*" [slang for parachutes] of you and your men in the sky over Shaba.

For that, mon Colonel, *MERCI.* As to all the rest (e.g., political criticism of action), treat it at its proper value.

Signed: Communist militant

An understanding of the problems faced by the 2nd REP and its commander at Kolwezi is necessary to appreciate fully the success of its action. In a long, confidential report to the general commanding the 11th Parachute Division, Colonel Erulin detailed the step-by-step preparation and unfolding of the operation with an eye to improving the procedures in the future.

"As important but calculated risks were taken under the circumstance," Erulin wrote, "I believe it necessary to treat with prudence the lessons learned by a Regiment operating far from its base." The colonel reported,

In general, *Bonite* was characterized by: the extreme rapidity of its organization, the speed of the reaction, the suppleness and adaptation shown by the participants in unusual circumstance, the importance and speed of the results obtained, due in part to luck but, above all, to the applied training of the personnel (night fighting in particular), their discipline and the confidence they have in their cadre, and their exceptional physical condition and endurance.

Some of the incidents in the colonel's report are classic examples of "Murphy's Law," applied to a military situation and based on the precept that anything that can go wrong, will go wrong. To begin with, the regiment's organization, "already calculated down to the line," called for forty-two (infantry) officers in the 2nd REP. At the moment of departure, twenty officers were on missions outside the regiment, including seven on operation in Chad and three taking a captain's course.

Under "prime difficulties" Erulin mentions "the lack of information on the fate of the European population . . . and the strength of the enemy." He also points out the lack of accurate, up-to-date maps as a major detriment that "could have caused dramatic problems" stating, "You can only carry out street fighting with recent directional maps or aerial photos in large number."

Colonel Erulin said the operation did prove that "perfectly trained troops" could adapt quickly to unforeseen circumstances. Upon arrival in Zaire, with only minutes to go, the regiment was equipped with American-made T-10 parachutes borrowed from the Zairian Army. The Legionnaires had never seen nor used the T-10s before. A hurried familiarization course on the Kinshasa airstrip with the help of some French military advisers serving with the Zairian Army, and former U.S. troopers in the Legion ranks, explained the basics of the new chutes, which were very different from French parachutes.

The Legion paras jump with their arms and equipment attached to their parachute harness by various buckles and clips. The American parachutes were without such accessories. The Legionnaires were thus forced to improvise makeshift attachments for the T-10 chutes with pliers, bits of wire, and strong twine.

Colonel Erulin cited "the excellent physical condition of all personnel" as their prime asset in enduring, "the fatigue resulting from two nights without sleep, the long voyage, the long wait in the military parking area of the Kinshasa airfield under a crushing heat, and the inevitable nervous tension preceding a jump into the unknown."

Under the heading "Problems of the Airdrop" the colonel spoke of frustrating delays and counterorders. The whole first wave was forced to disembark from the aircraft and shed their parachutes only to be ordered to reembark a short time later—and all of this under a punishing African sun. The normal prejump inspection of chutes by jumpmasters and fellow paras then became impossible owing to crowding aboard the aircraft. This crowding was aggravated when the engine of one Hercules transport failed, and its load of paras had to be divided and squeezed into the other aircraft. Another transport was found to have a deflated tire. At one point during the wait, the bored Zairian pilots strayed from the airstrip and had to be hunted down.

One incident duly reported by the colonel could have been fatal. Owing to the vagaries of the wind, aircraft movement, or equipment disfunction during the jump, a Legionnaire found himself hooked onto the transport's tail assembly by his static line. The horrified jumpmaster signaled that he was going to cut the line with his trench knife while gesturing desperately for the para to prepare his emergency chute. When the taut static line was cut, the experienced para cooly opened his emergency chute and cleared the aircraft safely. Miraculously, despite the do-it-yourself preparations on the airstrip, none of the paras lost his personal equipment.

The report continued:

- Errors in navigation by personnel of the Zaire Air Force added an hour to the planned length of the flight. One must underline the role of the crew chief aboard one C-160 who intervened to re-establish order in the formation commanded by a Zairian pilot obviously unfamiliar with his operational responsibilities.
- Despite what had been said, no fire support before the jump had been furnished by the Zairian (Air Force) Mirages. Due to a lack of ammunition, they only carried out intimidation passes.
- Without a photo of the drop zone, nor a radio-electronic aid on the ground, the formation had to pass over Kolwezi (town) to locate the DZ (thus giving the Tigers warning time to prepare their defense).

- Despite the request for a drop at 250 meters, the drops took place at heights ranging from 200 to 400 meters.
- The beginnings and end of the drops, often far from the DZ, made regroupment even more difficult (grass more than 2 meters high) and complicated the recuperation of collective equipment.
- The point of the drop was not always followed, thus dispersing personnel over a long distance.
- The drop was carried out in very difficult conditions: paras tired and overloaded (maximum munitions, four days' supply of radio batteries, two days' rations), high temperature, high ground wind, DZ hard and uneven. Accidents were, nevertheless, not too common (four fractures, two sprains).

The report discusses enemy organization, movements, and the presence of their foreign advisers on an inspection tour of Kolwezi on May 17. This information came from European residents "worthy of confidence."

Although Erulin's words are couched in the unemotional style of a military document, there is little doubt that no love was lost between the Belgian paracommandos and the 2nd REP. Speaking of coordination, or, rather, lack of coordination with the Belgian forces, the colonel reported:

> This important problem was not resolved until the afternoon of May 21. In fact, nothing could be planned before the arrival of the Belgians at Kolwezi on the morning of May 20. Despite the commander-to-commander liaison carried out by Colonel Gras (French Military Attaché in Kinshasa) and (Belgian) Colonel Depoorter at the airport, the Belgian units ignored the limits of their fixed zone of action: this was the origin of grave misunderstandings, particularly in Manika where the nervousness of our allies almost resulted in serious losses in our ranks.

Some veterans of the Kolwezi operation phrased it more directly, labeling the Belgians as obstinate, nervous, and trigger-happy. The Belgian paracommandos' animosity doubtless derived partly from their arrival in what had once been their own colonial territory too late for the main action. They found themselves, as an elite unit, assigned to evacuating liberated hostages and fulfilling police duties. Despite continued attempts to coordinate activities with the Belgians, Colonel Erulin finally decided to take unilateral action.

"As no attention was paid to the zone of action fixed in common," he explained, "the Colonel commanding the 2nd REP decided to avoid serious incidents and turn over the entire sector (Kolwezi town) to the Belgians from 1300 on May 20th." This left the 2nd REP free to continue its mop-up operations beyond Kolwezi.

Other irritants existed between the French and Belgians that were not mentioned in Erulin's report. Before the first wave of Legion paras had boarded the aircraft for the drop on Kolwezi, a Belgian news agency in Brussels announced that "French parachutists had been dropped on the city (of Kolwezi)." Considering the communications facilities available to the Tiger's Eastern Bloc advisers and the hours of flight time remaining before the Legion paras reached the DZ, this security gaffe could have had serious repercussions.

Once on the ground, the Belgian paracommandos were adamant that their prime task was to evacuate all Europeans by airlift quickly and depart themselves within a set time limit. To Colonel Erulin and his staff, this "forced" evacuation was the height of folly. It fueled continued panic among the local civilians, turned Kolwezi into a ghost town, and delayed the return to normalcy and constructive commerce.

If Franco-Belgian relations at Kolwezi were strained, Franco-American cooperation—despite the unappreciated peanut butter—appeared to proceed smoothly. Colonel Erulin's report makes special mention of the "remarkable organization of the U.S. Air Force elements involved."

Colonel Erulin did not mince words about the lack of support received from his higher headquarters. He regretted the fact that the regiment's movement had begun without its commander's (himself) having received any information on the political situation in Zaire nor "any directive or orientation" concerning his mission. He knew only that the regiment was headed for Zaire because of the operational code word "*Bonite.*"

"The necessary preparations could only be carried out in a general fashion," he wrote, "and thanks only to information found in the press."

The colonel's complaint list included:

- Poor liaison (slow and often nonexistent) with the Airborne Command.
- The rapid evolution, difficult to understand on the spot, of the political situation.
- The very brief content of the messages received from Paris "that often didn't permit us to understand the spirit of the orders and their political significance."
- The lack of information on the activities and exact plans of the Zairian Army.
- The advance information obtained by the press compared with that of those responsible for the operation: the fundamental options (cessation of our actions around Kolwezi, movement on Lubumbashi, relief by the African Force, details of the 2nd REP's return to France) "were known by the journalists between twelve and thirty-six hours before we received our orders."

In retrospect, this laundry list of "Particular Problems," each one bearing the seed of possible disaster, renders the 2nd REP's Kolwezi operation even more of an accomplishment. Colonel Erulin's report also provided a checklist for improvement as the regiment prepared itself for future operations.

Although the regiment's casualties at Kolwezi can officially be described as "light," the death of any Legionnaire is considered serious. It is of personal concern to his superiors, from the commander of the Foreign Legion to his company officers and supervisory noncoms. Although death is approached realistically as an inevitable result of professional soldiering, the mourning is no less real.

No one is more aware of this than the regimental *aumônier*, or chaplain. Father Merle is the current chaplain of the 2nd REP. A former professional soldier before entering the priesthood, he has been with the Foreign Legion for eight years. He did not volunteer to join the paras at the age of fifty-three, but accepted the assignment. French Army chaplains hold no rank but, as Merle explained, "We are equal in grade to the person with whom we are talking."

Although the regulations stated that parachute qualification ended at the age of forty-five, the chaplain decided that he could not be a nonjumper serving a regiment of paras. As paras tend basically to be an unconventional lot, the top brass looked the other way, as he passed through parachute school and earned his wings.

The doors of the chaplain's office at Camp Raffalli are open to all Legionnaires, regardless of their faith, needs, and problems. "I'm prepared to handle funeral services and eulogies for any religion," Father Merle explained. "It's more or less the same ceremony, but if the dead man is a Buddhist, I use the Buddhist Book of Wisdom, and, if Arab, the Koran." He pointed out that individual combat rations are available for Jews and Muslims.

The end of the cold war and an influx of Eastern Europeans into the Legion created a minor problem. "They are extremely positive about their religion," the Chaplain said, "but they expect and demand much incense, many candles, and ancient, traditional songs." Luckily, Father Merle, who has had some experience assisting at an Orthodox mass near Moscow, has been able to satisfy his new "parishioners."

Recently, he marked the twenty-fifth year of his priesthood by a solo pilgrimage on foot from Saint Madeleine de Vezelay in France to Santiago de Compostela in Spain. Booted, wearing a field uniform, and carrying a seventeen-kilo pack, the priest covered nineteen hundred kilometers in fifty-nine days.

This exploit is in the tradition of the famous *aumôniers* of the Legion—the bone-tired, haggard men who saw to the proper burial of the dead during fighting withdrawals in Tonkin and the dust-covered chaplains administering the last rites on the wind-swepped Djebels of Algeria.

A comparative period of peace brings no relief to the chaplains of the Legion. Father Merle's duties take him anywhere in the world that his Legionnaires are on duty or confronting death. Legion parachutists are not overly religious, and most treat religion as a very private matter that is seldom discussed. A simple poem from the archives of the French Army ground forces dating from World War II may closely echo the thoughts of some paras.

THE PARACHUTIST'S PRAYER

God, give me what you have left
Give me what no one ever requests.

I am not asking you for rest
Nor tranquility
Neither that of the soul, nor of the body.

I am not asking for wealth
Nor success, or even health.

You are asked for all of these so often
That you must have none left.

Give me, God, what you do have left.
Give me what no one wants.

I seek insecurity and disquiet.
I seek torment and combat
And, God, give them to me indefinitely.
That I am sure to have them always
Because I won't always have the courage to
Ask you.

Give me, God, what you have left.
Give me what others don't want.
But also give me courage, strength and faith.

André Zirnheld
Parachutiste, Free French Forces,
killed in action, 1942.

6

THE ELITE OF THE ELITE

They were our eyes and ears. They carried out scouting missions along the Burundi frontier. They cadred 150 Rwandan Gendarmerie troops, performed police actions and de-mining, acted as bodyguards, and rescued a government minister. They were flexible, of top quality, and at the right place at the right time.

> Lt. Colonel Jacques Hogard, Legion recruiting chief, recalling the CRAP Team that worked with him in Rwanda.

Like most military aircraft, the interior of the Transall C-160 is strictly utilitarian, a cigar tube of shiny metal, canvas seats and straps, collapsible ladders, stenciled emergency instructions, and gleaming overhead metal wires. The rows of paras slump in their seats, facing each other, knee to knee, helmets low on their heads, chin straps taut. Their chutes prevent their settling into a comfortable position. Many are dozing, some are staring straight ahead, and a few are joking among themselves. The jumpmasters are checking stored equipment or talking to the flight crew on their intercoms.

I am squeezed between two husky paras and the bulk of their chutes. I recognize a German noncom who helped me on the pistol range a few days earlier, and we exchange a few words before the engines start. Further conversation is now impossible. The turboprop engines roar and the Transall shimmies, hanging on its brakes like an old C-47. Then we surge forward, moving over the tarmac, gaining speed with an occasional hard thump, and finally lifting off, edging into a sweeping turn over Calvi and the curved shoreline of the bay.

It was not easy to obtain permission to embark with the jumpers of the 2nd REP. The Legion has previously had some problems with writers and media representatives, including those with preconceived ideas, determined to produce sensationalism or a hatchet job. There is also the risk of involving a visiting civilian in an accident with attendant medical or legal complications. Fortunately, someone in authority in Paris, Aubagne, or Calvi had made the decision that I was a good risk. This was not the first time I had witnessed an airdrop of French paras, but I still followed my own basic rule—watch but do not jump. This has become more important as the years flow by.

The young paras eyed me with some curiosity, but Legionnaires are not given to either idle curiosity or probing questions. To them, I was *le journaliste* or *l'Américain*. They had other preoccupations at the moment, such as sleeping, daydreaming, or checking their equipment. A member of the flight crew swung down from the steps leading to the cockpit and offered me a seat with the pilots. I declined, lifting my camera to indicate that I intended to photograph the paras as they left the Transall.

A sudden bout of turbulence had us bucking and yawing. The jumpmasters near the unopened doors grabbed for support and exchanged grins. At this point the man across from me began to roll his eyes. He leaned forward and moaned slightly. I thought I could see perspiration on his forehead. The para on his right turned to examine his companion.

"*Oh merde!*" he shouted, "he's airsick again and he's going to vomit!"

I might have panicked if I had had any room to maneuver but there was none. I was knee to knee with the apparently stricken Legionnaire. His face was a foot from my own, and I could not move left nor right. He was now making an apparent effort to keep his breakfast down, gulping and swallowing. I watched helplessly as he finally lurched toward me with a loud "Aaaarrrgh!" and feigned the act of being sick.

I'd been had. The Legionnaire was no more sick than I was. I was neither the first, nor last, outsider to have fallen for this old para joke. Judging from the chuckles and smiles around me I had been a perfect patsy. I can only imagine how big my eyes had become under such a threat. When I joined in the laughter, it was more from relief than from any benevolent humor.

The opening of the doors signaled the beginning of the drop run. Bright sunlight suddenly flooded the interior of the Transall, and a cold wind buffeted the jumpmasters as they leaned out to locate the DZ. All around me the sleepers awakened, and a sergeant put away his nail clippers.

"*Debout! Accrochez!*," "Standup! Hookup!," a jumpmaster bellowed.

I was suddenly in deep shadow as all the paras rose to clip their static lines onto the overhead wires. I moved along the cot-like, canvas seats to the starboard door, while the paras performed a last-minute chute check of the men in front of them. The jumpmasters moved along the line, verifying the static lines. A jumpmaster by the door cast a quick, puzzled glance in my direction as I readied my camera.

The red light flashed on, and the file of paras pushed closer together. After a short wait, a strident, insistent buzzer sounded, the light changed to green, and the jumpmaster's shout of "Go!" was almost lost in a blast of wind. Never before had I seen a transport empty so quickly. The Legionnaires left the aircraft as though they were joined together. Liberated from their weight, the Transall rose in the clear air, and the jumpmasters began hauling the flapping lines into the nearly empty aircraft. It was nice to have some space.

We climbed higher, and I noted that we had not turned back toward Calvi. A jumpmaster noticed my puzzled look. Using sign language, he explained that they had one more drop before their job was done. A small group of paras was seated near the opposite door. They were wearing banded goggles over bright red, soft jump helmets. Their lower legs were wrapped in leggings of the same hue. Altimeters were strapped to their wrists. One para was kneeling in the open doorway, peering intently at the ground through the light cover of drifting clouds.

These were men of the regiment's commando team, *les Commandos de Recherche et d'Action dans le Profondeur* (CRAP). Their exercise of the day involved a HALO (High Altitude-Low Opening) drop on a DZ representing a small airstrip and its seizure for subsequent occupation by a larger force. The Transall climbed higher, and the crewmen activated the opening mechanism for the wide rear door. Two of the paracommandos were carrying on a shouted conversation on the use of arm and leg positions in controlling a free fall.

We were now approaching the DZ, and the commandos moved toward the gaping exit. I followed, and the jumpmasters indicated where I should stand. I settled into position with my chest braced on a metal stanchion, readied my camera, and felt a hard tap on the shoulder. Sergeant Lance Phillips, a New Zealander and regimental photographer doubling as a jumpmaster, handed me a parachute.

"What's this for?" I shouted over the engine din.

"You can jump with them."

"Oh, no." I replied, refusing the proffered chute.

"The colonel's approved it."

"I don't give a s . . . !," I replied in desperation, my voice betraying a certain panic.

We stood there for several seconds pushing the chute back and forth. Then the broad smiles of Phillips and the other jumpmasters told me I'd been had for the second time. They did insist that I don the chute but only as a safety precaution. Its bulk proved reassuring, as I stood close to the door with a jumpmaster gripping my belt and watched the *chuteurs opérationnels* launch themselves into the void like Olympic divers.

The day after my airborne experience, one of the Transalls got into trouble as it took off for its home base and made a crash landing on the nearby mountain. Luckily, there were no paras aboard, and the pilots' skill produced a miracle. They put the heavy transport down between the two rock ridges of a mountain, its nose pointing up the steep slope toward the crest. There had been no fire nor excessive breakup, and the aircrew had suffered only a broken arm and collarbone. It was not difficult to imagine what might have happened, if the Transall had been fully loaded with its full complement of fifty-eight paras.

Once the exercises were over, I sat down with Captain Bruno Schiffer and his staff to discuss the organization and work of his CRAP teams. The elite of the elite, these twenty-five officers and noncoms are divided into two teams of ten men each plus a command group. The first free-fall special jumpers were formed in 1970, but the organization of the regular commando units began in 1980. All parachute regiments in the 11th Parachute Division now have one or two CRAP teams. All are trained to work in support of the regiment and its companies, either with other CRAP teams in a divisional framework, or alone on special operations. Although the *Direction Général de la Sécurité Extérieure* (DGSE), France's CIA, can call on the CRAP teams of the 11th Parachute Division for assistance in specific classified operations, most such confidential work is handled by the specially trained paras of the 11th CHOC.

Legion paras are recruited as volunteers for the commando teams after they have completed two or three years' service and hold the rank of corporal. They then undergo intense commando training in the Pyrenees. Once they have passed the required medical and mental tests, the Legionnaires are sent to the parachute center at Pau to become qualified as *chuteurs opérationnels* or operational jumpers.

The commandos of the 2nd REP tend to be more mature than the men of the average Legion unit. The two officers and the noncoms of CRAP are from twenty-eight to thirty years of age. Currently, the majority of these special soldiers are of Italian, Spanish, or British origin with few Germans or Americans in their ranks. They are all members of a very close-knit team. Their operational interdependence as commandos appears to have erased the barriers of rank without affecting efficiency.

Although the regiment's Combat Companies are trained for a particular field of warfare, the individual commandos of CRAP must each be qualified in certain basic specialities—as a commando instructor, a military mountaineer and skier, a reconnaissance swimmer, a sharpshooter, and so forth. In addition, from the moment a new member arrives, he is integrated into a team and personally specialized in one of the following fields—as a medic, radio-man, tactical photographer, demolition or intelligence expert, auto mechanic, or expert in hand-to-hand combat. A document on the CRAP teams mentions that "the training followed is intense and rigorous." Considering what I observed, this borders on understatement.

Most of the CRAP team's missions can be divided into intelligence operations, offensive actions, and specific actions. Intelligence operations include: gathering information on the enemy's strength and progress and on enemy deployment in a specific zone; gathering information on a military objective or infrastructure; and gathering information on a situation and an environment.

Offensive actions include: the seizure and temporary control of a key point; preparations for the deployment of a larger force (pathfinding); destruction of objectives within enemy lines; neutralization or destruction of infrastructure objectives; participation in controlling a zone; establishing a climate of insecurity in an enemy area; and the extraction of those under threat.

Specific actions include: searching for, finding, regrouping, and evacuating French and allied citizens; antisniping; military assistance; and providing protection for those in authority.

While the paracommando is no stranger to long-range penetration patrols, antitank warfare, and directing artillery fire and air support, he must also learn to put together a dossier covering targets or zones of possible future interventions. This means gathering material and absorbing details on the geography, economy, politics, ethnic composition, and traditions of specific operational areas.

The specialists of CRAP are constantly on the go. To keep fit for operations, they jump anywhere in Corsica at all hours, conduct amphibious landings, scale snowy peaks, or slide rapidly earthward from hovering choppers. Equipped with special, directional chutes, they can navigate laterally to a specific objective and land ten men within a ninety-meter square following a HALO drop.

Not all drops are so precise. I watched a CRAP team drift slowly toward a ground marker on the Camp Raffalli DZ, while a smoke grenade spewed its contents to indicate wind direction. The first stick of jumpers was dropped too late, but the men fought hard to maneuver their chutes as close as possible to the dark bullseye on the ground target. The senior jumpmaster "the Bear," was watching the drop through a tripod scope and shaking his head and lamenting, "Too far! Too far!"

Only one para, an experienced officer, managed to hit the marker. "*Largage ZERO!*" he shouted to the jumpmaster. He was in a murderous mood, cursing aloud as he doused his chute. He swore at the pilots for overshooting the DZ and at the Air Force for producing such cretins. Then he bellowed at his scattered men to join him, "*Allez, vite!*" he shouted, checking his watch, "We've got time to try it again."

The second drop was just as bad and even farther off target. The furious "Bear" gathered his equipment and stamped off the DZ to his office, walking past a group of apprentice trumpeters and drummers practicing the refrain of "Le Boudin." "I've already moved my office once to escape that racket!," he growled.

Air Force Transalls fly into Calvi from their mainland base at Evreux to work with the 2nd REP. During their stay, the Legion lays on some orientation functions to explain its work and objectives. Such understanding is important for a smooth operational partnership between paras and the aircrews. This is particularly vital regarding the CRAP teams as the aircrews could be involved with the commandos in sensitive infiltration and exfiltration operations.

The same briefings are arranged for the aircrews of the *Aviation Légère Armée de Terre* (ALAT)—the chopper pilots and light aircraft support of the Army Ground Forces. After a closed session in a Camp Raffalli lecture hall, the aircrews inspect CRAP equipment displayed outdoors on ground sheets and question the Legion commandos about their work and weapons.

The standard commando weapon is the Heckler & Koch submachine gun (H&K SMG) with laser sights and silencer. Weapons are chosen according to the job to be done, but most commandos carry three weapons each. In addition to the H&K SMG, the CRAP armory includes: the 9mm Beretta automatic pistol, the pump action 12-gauge shotgun with pistol grip, the FR-FI 7.26mm sniper's rifle, and the .50 caliber Barrett (long-range) sniper's rifle, a variety of grenades, and individual fighting knives.

The aircrews move among the displays and crouch down to heft the weapons as the Legionnaires describe their use and capabilities. One commando, completely fitted out for a tactical jump, is wearing night goggles and a chest-high control panel for self-navigation, including a compass, altimeter, and speed indicator. The additional weight of his chutes, weapons, ammunition, and rations soon has him sagging, until he braces his back against a nearby wall. In addition to their own armament, all CRAP members are trained in the use of foreign weapons, a useful, life-preserving skill in the hard, unforgiving world of unconventional warfare.

A young *caporal-chef* wearing the gold stars of an operational jumper on his wings was among the paracommandos I spoke with at Camp Raffalli. He had served three years as a para in the regular army, including a six-month tour in Gabon. This had taught him "bush survival" and introduced him to the debilitation of malaria. He had found the Legion quite different: the mix of foreigners, more mature soldiers, and changes in training. He had been assigned to the 1st Company (street fighting/antitank) and completed the jungle training course in French Guiana. He had then served in Rwanda, Chad, and Togo. He had participated in the Gulf campaign with the regiment's CRAP team. His decorations included the croix de guerre (overseas) with bronze star; the Overseas Commemoration Medal with bars for Lebanon, Chad, Middle East, and Somalia; the Kuwait Liberation Medal, and the Saudi Arabian Medal for the Kuwait campaign.

On the principle that clichés often prove to be true, I had expected to meet a larger-than-life, hard-case commando. Instead the *caporal-chef* proved to be soft-spoken, even shy, and particularly modest about his career and experiences.

A more senior member of the 2nd REP's commandos gave me a perfect description of his team's worth in describing a recent assignment. In July 1994, the prime minister of Rwanda, Dismas Nsengiyareme, was under surveillance in his residence surrounded by members of the Rwanda Army. The prime minister, a Tutsi, had suggested putting some moderate Hutus in his government. This was "taken badly" by Rwandan Army leaders who were then conducting a lethal "hunt for moderates" throughout the country. The French ambassador took the threat to the prime minister seriously and called for protection. A CRAP team of ten men conducted a daylight chopper raid to rescue the prime minister and his family. There was no shooting, and the Rwanda Army troops were quickly dominated "without breakage." "They knew who [*sic*] they were dealing with," my interlocuter explained.

Operation *Epaulard* (Grampus) in August-September of 1982 sent the 2nd REP under Lt. Colonel Janvier to Beirut as the spearhead of a multinational force to support the "Habib Plan" for peace in the Middle East. For the Legion, it was a return to historically familiar ground, as both Lebanon and Syria came under French mandate after World War I. During World War II, France's Vichy government retained control until 1941, when a British and Free French force landed on the Lebanese coast to assume temporary wartime power in both countries.

The regiment's 1st and 2nd companies, in addition to a headquarters group supported by a CRAP Team, flew to Cyprus on August 18 and 19. They then boarded French naval vessels for the voyage to Beirut where they docked early on the morning of August 21. The paras were charged with a delicate mission in a tinderbox atmosphere. Beirut was a battle-damaged moonscape filled with hate and rival armed factions, most of whom had deep reservations about the international peace effort.

The Israeli Army with its four armored and mechanized divisions; the

"Progressive Palestinians" with nine thousand fighting men; the Palestinian Liberation Army of fourteen hundred; the Syrian Army with a Brigade of twenty-five hundred men; the Lebanese Left with four thousand fighters; and the battered and often humiliated National Army of Lebanon—these were the battle-hardened players on the ground.

The 2nd REP was entering the game with carefully delineated responsibilities. The regiment was to ensure the physical security of the Palestinians as they withdrew from Beirut; see that the Palestinian departure was conducted properly under the direction of the Lebanese Army; support the Lebanese Army, help the civilian population, and secure the residence of the French ambassador.

From 0545 on August 21, the Legion paras moved to take control of their first objective—the commercial port of Beirut. Despite the hostility of some Israeli troops who objected to evacuating their positions, and the time spent in relieving Palestinians and Syrians, the port was under Legion control and isolated by 1100.

For the next week, the paras supervised the evacuation of over thirty-four hundred Palestinians. This was a nerve-racking task, as each seaborne departure was signaled by a celebratory firestorm of automatic weapons, recoilless rifles, and even rocket-propelled grenades. This dangerous form of exuberance cost the lives of a number of people, and many others were wounded by stray projectiles.

Relieved at the port by the U.S. Marines, the 2nd REP moved on to the "Green Line," where it replaced units of the Palestinian Liberation Army. The paras also reclaimed the abandoned, shell-battered French embassy in central Beirut, swept it for mines, and returned it to a grateful French ambassador.

On August 30, the CRAP team of the 2nd REP was handed one of the most sensitive jobs in Beirut. These paracommandos, acting as bodyguards for Palestinian leader Yassir Arafat, had to escort him from his heavily fortified headquarters, through the menace-filled streets, to the ship taking him to Cyprus. In addition, their special missions included the scuba-diving inspection of the ship's hulls for mines before embarking the Palestinians.

On September 13, 1982—after more patrols, civic action, and continued support of the Lebanese Army—the 2nd REP climbed aboard *super-Frelon* helicopters to be lifted to the aircraft carrier *Foch* for the trip back to Calvi. The international force of French, American, and Italian troops had seen to the evacuation from Lebanon of nine thousand fedayeen irregulars, twenty-five hundred troops of the Palestine Liberation Army and a two thousand-man contingent of the Syrian Army. Such figures can only reflect part of this accomplishment. Considering the tensions, prevalence of weapons, and lack of discipline often displayed by the combatants, it was a miracle the evacuations occurred without a major clash. Much of this was owing to the professionalism and steadiness of the international force, including the men of the 2nd REP.

Corsica has been a political powderkeg for years thanks to the Corsican National Liberation Front (FLNC) and other nationalist splinter groups. These are not romantic vestiges of Corsica's violent past but hard-core revolutionary groups using explosives and firearms to attack, maim, and kill French police and officials and to destroy French installations. They have also mounted campaigns against foreigners seeking the Mediterranean sun and a vacation villa on the "Isle of Beauty." The burned-out hulks of expensive holiday homes are no novelty in Corsica.

The road from Calvi to Camp Raffalli runs alongside a destroyed holiday apartment complex. It appears the foreign owner did not seek the right "permission" before construction. The 2nd REP has occasionally used the lugubrious empty complex for house-to-house fighting exercises.

The night of my arrival in Calvi, a bomb exploded on the façade of a bank about two thousand yards from where I was sleeping at the Cercle Sampiero within the Citadel. I slept through the entire episode but awakened to find that it had been but one of thirty-four explosions throughout the island that night.

Strangely enough, the 2nd REP's base at Camp Raffalli has been an island of calm in the midst of this militant unrest. True, Colonel Erulin's sedan was bombed with no casualties shortly after the Kolwezi operation, but the cause is still hazy and the perpetrators unclear. So far, the FLNC and the 2nd REP appear to coexist through an unwritten rule of noninterference by both parties. The Legion is not involved in security operations against the FLNC, leaving that to the police, the Gendarmerie, and the *Direction de la Surveillance du Territoire* (DST). The FLNC is probably aware that any attack on Legionnaires would be unpopular with the many Corsicans who have economic and personal links with the Legion. More important, they know the Legion well enough to realize that any such action would not go unpunished. In October 1995, the FLNC announced a truce with the rival group "Movement for Self-Determination." Their feud had cost twelve dead in nine months. The truce was touted as "an answer to the deep yearnings for peace of the Corsican people." If such "yearnings" could be applied to the FLNC's independence struggle, the island's security forces—and the Legion—would breathe a deep sigh of relief. Alas, more violent deaths during December 1995 and early 1996 showed that the internal quarrels were far from over.

Camp Raffalli is surrounded by barbed wire, patrolled by dog handlers with their *chiens de guerre* (war dogs), and kept under observation by sentries in an unused jump tower. From their own operational experience, however, the paras know that security is never perfect. During my stay, the CRAP team conducted a night helicopter descent on the camp to test the regiment's defenses and nocturnal teamwork with the choppers. I was told that the operation exposed numerous weaknesses that would be remedied.

The two security officers on the base run their own military police patrols charged with security and prevention in and around Calvi, but they do not become involved in law enforcement. That is the task of the local police and gendarmerie. Considering that Legionnaires are far from being choir boys and have been exposed to a certain amount of violence during their service, there are surprisingly few cases of violent drunks misbehaving outside the camp. The bar owners in Calvi call the regimental security office directly in the event of expected trouble.

Recently, an influx of hard-drinking Eastern Europeans, unaccustomed to a western environment, has caused some problems. The security officer, however, described the majority of the new paras as "hardworking" men who "save money rather than drink it." He cited some paras who had saved enough money in the Legion after three years to buy their own businesses in Poland.

Like all Legion units, the 2nd REP is very hard on drug users. Even if narcotics are used "outside," the risk of "contamination" is considered too great, and users are asked to leave. Alcoholism is also discouraged, but sufferers are often given help and a chance to reform. If this fails, they, too, become former Legionnaires. "We settle our own problems," I was told.

Desertion is a reality that security officers have to live with. It is less of a problem now than it was in the past, but disillusion, an aversion to discipline, troubles at home, romantic entanglements, and the inability to adapt to a different language and environment can be the causes. Group desertions by comrades of the same nationality were not unknown in the old Legion, and tribal bounty hunters often returned them—or their heads—for a profit. During the Indochina War, sentries kept watch for Legionnaires plunging into the water as outgoing troop ships passed close to shore. Today's Legion paras, as two-time volunteers, are less likely to go over the fence.

The Legion remains alert to the possibility of plants or sleepers from foreign intelligence services. The ongoing turmoil in Eastern Europe and the Balkans has made it particularly hard for security officers to obtain solid information on new recruits from those regions.

Before their arrival at Camp Raffalli, the new paras will have already passed through three weeks of physical examinations, I.Q. and psychological testing at Legion Headquarters in Aubagne. This, in addition to their sixteen weeks of basic training with the 4th Regiment at Castelnaudary, provide security officers time to follow the recruit's progress and to receive replies to information requested from non-Legion sources.

"The ideal recruit," a security officer said with a sigh, "would be an eighteen-year-old without prior experience in other armies," indicating the Legion preferred to train new recruits in its own methods.

The regimental security office maintains good relations with the civic and police authorities in Corsica, but that does not mean that its officers remain within the confines of the camp. "A good security officer must know the local environment," a professional told me. "He must listen carefully to word-of-mouth information. Nothing is done without good intelligence."

The truth of that statement became apparent one Sunday morning while I was sipping an espresso on a café terrace overlooking the Bay of Calvi and reading *La Corse Dimanche*. This Corsican edition of the Marseille newspaper *Le Provençal* had broken a story that would turn a security officers' hair gray overnight, but it proved that the 2nd REP's guardians were alert and functioning.

Arms Shipment Seized

Since January the Nice police, the Police Judiciare of Ajaccio and the DST have followed leads on arms traffic that led them to suspect a Legionnaire who—while acting as the temporary supervisor of the 2nd REP's armory—was regularly removing arms. The Legion's security officers intercepted an impressive shipment of anti-tank mines, grenades, plastic explosives, and rocket launching tubes with warheads.

The *Caporal-Chef* in question, aided by an accomplice, removed enough arms and munitions to fill a truck for loading onto a cargo ship in the Bay of Calvi. These included over 1,000 offensive grenades, 1,000 defensive grenades, 500 kilos of explosives, and thousands of cartridges including 5,000 of 9mm.

The truck was stopped by Legion security as it left the Camp. François Leotard, the Minister of Defense, and Charles Pasqua, the Minister of the Interior, were aware of the dossier. The local police are not happy with Legion security as they wanted to follow the shipment bound for the *milieu Niçoise* (the Nice underworld) to find the dealers. According to the police much of the shipment was meant for Algeria.

Having had experience with Drug Enforcement Agency tracking methods while serving as U.S. Consul General in Marseille, I understood the frustration of the police. But I could also understand the security officers' desire to keep such a heavy haul of lethal cargo within the walls of Camp Raffalli and in Legion hands.

Much has changed in the Legion since the days when new officers were warned that discipline could be maintained only through an iron hand, frequent imprisonment, and a regime of brutal punishment. The "men without names" who served in North Africa between the two World Wars often experienced beatings, long exposure without water under a fiery sun, solitary confinement, and punishment marches.

As recently as 1962, former British Legionnaire Simon Murray wrote of the punishments meted out to his 2nd REP Platoon in Algeria for smashing up the plates and glasses in a company mess tent. The result—thirty days in prison for the plate smashers with harsher penalties for the noncoms.

"Kroll has been made to sign a paper forfeiting his parachute *brevet* and he is thrown out of the Regiment, stripped of his rank and collects fifteen days' prison in the bargain. This in spite of the fact that he is one of the most highly decorated men in the company. He has the *Médaille Militaire* and the *Croix de Valeur Militaire* with three stars and a palm. Starry, who was going to Corporal School, has been banned forever so that he can never rise above the rank of private." Murray then expressed his belief that the officers had overreacted and that the punishment had been unnecessarily harsh. "For the rest," he wrote, "the *refectoire* (mess hall) is closed and we are to take our meals standing to attention in the sun and we are on hard labor from sun-up to sun-down until further notice. In addition we have a barrack and kit inspection every morning and evening."

Today the Legion adheres to the same basic regulations regarding punishment as the French Regular Army. Legionnaires are now more exposed to the outside world than they were when stationed in isolated desert outposts. Each new recruit reflects his own individual historical and cultural background and the mores of the civilian environment he has left behind.

One experienced officer who had attended a training program in the United States claimed the Legion was "not as violent as the U.S. Army" with fewer on and off-post fights. He stated that punishment was not as it used to be and that beatings were a thing of the past. "True," he said, "military prisoners still work from dawn until dusk, but look at them." He gestured toward a group of fatigue-clad prisoners cleaning up a nearby flower bed. "Damn gardeners," he remarked disdainfully.

This is not to say that the Legion has dropped its hard rocks for a complement of cream puffs. Legion discipline, if fair, is still severe. Although unauthorized, some noncoms may still consider their fists to be disciplinary tools. Combat troops of any nation—and paras in particular—become edgy and belligerent during long stretches of garrison duty. Luckily for the 2nd REP, its numerous overseas duty assignments and realistic training exercises provide the needed safety valve.

One section of the regiment that began as a security support function has now expanded to fulfill other duties. During the 1980s, the 2nd REP obtained a canine unit primarily to patrol Camp Raffalli's perimeter. Since then, after passing through the two-month course of the Army Ground Force dog train-

ing center with their handlers, the four-legged "Legionnaires" are now qualified for guard duty, scouting, tracking, searching for explosives, and attack
functions.

"Diabolo," "Hanoi," "Silax," "Echo," and "Motu" are only a few of the
German shepherds and Rotweillers among the thirteen "war dogs" currently
serving with the 2nd REP. That number is expected to reach twenty-five in a
year's time. The platoon's leader supervises thirteen handlers and thirteen
male dogs. These animals from northern France, Belgium, Holland, and Germany are selected at one or one and one-half years of age for their intelligence
and aggressiveness.

The intensive training has taught the dogs to bark or to attack only when
so ordered. Their reactions to explosions, gunfire, and the threat of a club
have all been tested. The handlers claim their dogs' night vision is "excellent"
up to 200 meters and feed them a daily ration of 800 grams of dehydrated,
high-protein food. "These are working animals," they explain.

While talking with the dog handlers, I inadvertently cut a corner that took
me close to a large, sitting German shepherd. The low rumble of a growl and
bared teeth froze me in my tracks. A quick reprimand from the handler
calmed him. "These are highly nervous animals," I was told. "Never approach
or pet them when their handler is not present." This was definitely superfluous
advice, as far as I was concerned.

In October 1994, the canine platoon joined the 1st Company. They now
are present during most of the company's activities, including firing exercises,
marches, flights, and street-fighting operations—the company's speciality. A
recent demonstration drill had two dog teams supporting a platoon attack on
a group of fortified dwellings, which impressed visiting brass from the 11th
Parachute Division.

A special sling has been devised that allows a dog to travel on the back of
his handler as he rappels down the sheer face of a mountain or steep wall.
Work is progressing on equipment that would provide a fail-safe method for
the dogs to pass their parachute qualification and join the regiment jumping
into a live, operational DZ.

When a dog becomes too old or "too difficult," he is offered to his handler
as a pet or put up for civilian sale as a watchdog. In most cases, the long links
between dog and handler lead to the animal's adoption as a pet. Others are
snapped up as watchdogs by Corsican farmers or landowners. Those with
combat fatigue or "real psychological problems" must be put down.

Leaving the barking war dogs behind at dusk, I walked back toward Camp
Raffalli's headquarter's building. The setting sun was a shimmering orange
wrapped in a thin veil of purple cloud. A stiff wind was blowing in from the

sea. It occurred to me that with all my appointments and peregrinations, I had not yet explored the camp on my own. I pulled the sheet outlining my *programme possible* from my pocket and ran my finger over the day-to-day activities: "Firing with the 3rd Company," "CEA Platoon Training," "Mortar exercise with helicopters." There it was. I knew the last item was out. The helicopters had been canceled because of weather. This meant I could spend the day exploring Camp Raffalli.

7

RWANDA TO IRAQ

> The exact location of their encampment is a secret. But they are
> closer to the Iraqi lines than those of probably any other force.
>
> Report on the Foreign Legion during the Gulf War:
> *Sunday Times* (London), February 1991.

My day started out well. Orange juice, strong coffee, and a croissant at the *Caserne Sampiero*, a quick ride to Camp Raffalli, and a brief consultation with Major Bruno Brottier about my schedule. I was then on my own. First order of business—a haircut. Since my arrival in Calvi, what was left of my hair had grown into two wispy clusters, lending the aspect of a mad professor. This image did not fit easily into an environment where most of the inhabitants sported a short top and sides.

Directed to a Legion barber plying his trade at the CEA barracks, I asked the unbelieving Pole to "take it all off." He hesitated, shrugged, and switched on his electric clippers. Under the suprised gaze of his para customers, he proceeded to give me a *boule à zéro*, the standard skull skim for Legion recruits. There was no doubt about it. I would now fit into the local scene, even if more vulnerable to the sharp wind blowing from the mountains.

I paused on my way to the armory to watch a bandsman-instructor conducting an outdoor class with three apprentice buglers. He stood before a blackboard inscribed with the music of "Le Boudin," while his students struggled to coordinate their discordant efforts. Shaking his head, he waved them quiet, lifted his own bugle, and demonstrated how it should be done.

"It's easy," he told them, using the time-honored words of musical instructors everywhere, "Now, let's try it again." These blasts from the brass played to a steady rat-a-tat-tat from four nearby drummers attempting to learn their new speciality.

Caporal-Chef B welcomed me to the regimental armory. He is an American, a former U.S. Marine—a big, muscular man. He is also a knowledgeable mastercraftsman when it comes to the upkeep and repair of weapons of all types and provenance. I had first met B shortly after my arrival while he was carrying out adjustments to a mobile 20mm antiaircraft cannon. We had exchanged only a few words, but I had had the definite impression that he was in no hurry to chat with another American. Since then, things had become more relaxed, and we had always stopped to exchange a few words when our paths crossed in the camp.

The well-secured repair shop smelled of gun oil, cosmoline, and solvent. Weapons of all kinds were under repair or receiving new parts on the work tables. *Caporal-Chef* B offered me a black coffee and a briefing on the Legion's weapons. He was enthusiastic about the FR-FI 7.62 mm (NATO) sniper's rifle that "can put ten rounds in a small bullseye at 200 meters . . . with good ammunition." He classed the French standard machine gun as better than the U.S. M-60 but slightly heavier. The Legion's 50-caliber machine gun, mortars, and MILAN antitank missiles were all described as "tops." B found the 9mm MAB (*Manufacture d'Armes de Bayonne*) automatic pistol an acceptable weapon, but my notes on his comments are a bit sketchy, probably owing to my dismal firing record with that handgun earlier.

Putting weapons aside for a more general conversation, *Caporal-Chef* B made a special point of praising the chopper pilots of ALAT (*Aviation Légère Armée de Terre*) who often put the paras on the ground during operations and came in to take them out when summoned.

"The pilots of ALAT are better than their U.S. counterparts," B told me bluntly, "and more mature. Their choppers are excellent. The pilots can hang on a ridge top in a high wind. You can depend on them."

Leaving *Caporal-Chef* B with his weapons, I walked out into bright sunlight. The sea mist had cleared, the air was fresh, and a platoon of paras was marching past on its way to jump training. I pondered the role of Americans in the Legion as I waited for them to pass. I had been told that ten to twenty Americans joined the Legion annually. For many, their service preference seemed to be the 2nd REP. Some sought out the Legion for "real soldiering." This does not mean that they all received the regimental assignments requested.

During the late 1980s, while visiting Legion Headquarters at Aubagne in a car with California license plates, I had found a note on the windshield. "*Bonjour,*" it read, "I am from Yuba City, California, and could not help noticing your plates. Just wanted to say hello. Legionnaire Robert R. Lewis." I found Lewis later, working on the staff of *Képi Blanc*, the Legion magazine, and we exchanged memories of the California Sierras.

So far, I had met two American members of the 2nd REP: the bluff B, whom I had just left, and the reflective *Caporal-Chef* Ofria. One other para had been pointed out as a countryman, but he obviously wanted to avoid my company. I believe there were others in the regiment, but I had no desire to intrude on their privacy.

The military historian Lt. Col. Henry Dutailly, writing about foreign officers serving in the Legion, mentions "a family member of the Vice President of the Southern Confederacy" who joined during the Civil War period. By 1915, before the United States entered World War I, a number of Americans had become Legionnaires to fight under the French flag. Of the 3,314 noncoms who fought with the Legion from 1914 to 1918, 6.06 percent were Americans.

Perhaps the most famous American in Legion ranks during World War I was the poet Alan Seeger. Fresh out of Harvard and in a self-confessed search for glory, he joined a number of other American volunteers in *le Régiment de Marche de la Légion Étrangère* (RMLE). This regiment, a hybrid formed from the remnants of Legion units shattered by high casualties, became the most decorated unit of the French Army in World War I. A fierce five-day battle in July 1916 cost the regiment 869 dead. Among them was Legionnaire Seeger who had recently written "I Have a Rendezvous with Death"—a poem that would become a wartime classic. Two years later, composer and song writer Cole Porter joined the same regiment for a brief period of service.

One American occupies a special place in the crypt of the Legion in the museum at Aubagne along with the engraved lists of the Legion's dead and the retired battle flags of its former regiments. A small, polished wall plaque marks the resting place of William Moll from Chicago who died in 1937. Moll, who had served five years in the Legion, asked to be buried at Sidi-bel-Abbès. When the Legion left Algeria, his ashes were transferred to Aubagne.

No mention of Americans and the Legion can ignore the role played by Hollywood in turning rough service in the pre-World War II Legion into a romantic myth. The British author P. C. Wren's adventure novel, *Beau Geste*, was made and remade into films in 1926, 1931 ("Beau Ideal"), 1939, and 1966. In 1930, Marlene Dietrich and Legionnaire Gary Cooper exchanged smouldering glances and passionate kisses under the direction of Josef Von Sternberg in the film "Morocco." In 1939, Laurel and Hardy had a crack at Legion life in "Flying Deuces." More recently, Gene Hackman put on a Legion officer's uniform in "March or Die" to fight the Arabs as well as Catherine Deneuve's leaden performance. A recent advertisement on British television had a Legion officer and his sergeant buried up to their necks in desert sand for refusing their men a helping of Crunchy Nut Corn Flakes.

Leaving further musings on Americans for another time, I walked through a well-kept garden of lawns and flower beds ringed with cyprus, acacia, and pine. It led to *le Foyer du Legionnaire,* the equivalent of a PX-cum-enlisted man's club. The one-story, tile-roofed foyer includes a shop, a snack bar, bar, recreational facilities, and a cinema-theater. A small building nearby houses a video rental facility. A notice on the bulletin board lists family shopping hours each day from 1000 to 1130 hrs and announces that "children's haircuts (girls or boys)" are available Wednesday afternoon between 1400 and 1700 hours.

Observing family shopping in the foyer is to be reminded that many of the tough noncoms encountered during service hours also have a domestic side to their lives. Nor are wives and children barred from participation in on-base activities. The officer and noncom's messes at Camp Raffalli are open to Legion families on Sunday at noon, on holidays, and every evening beginning at 1900 hours.

Later during my stay, returning to the *Caserne Sampiero* late one afternoon, I found the ancient fortress echoing with children's shouts and the clatter of little feet on the wide stone steps. I had blundered onto a costume party; a gaggle of pirates, princesses, witches, Arab sheiks, and small, uniformed cavaliers with painted mustaches. I took some pleasure at finding a few para officers—so unflappable and stern before their men—looking harried and *fatigué* as they tried to control their highly charged offspring.

The life of a Legion wife is not easy. They are well aware of the risks their husbands take and are accustomed to sudden departures and long absences. Like service wives anywhere, they band together for mutual support through social activities, good works, and the special *fêtes* of the Legion. Although most of them appreciate the beauty and the beaches of Corsica, they quickly become aware that the city of Calvi is, in reality, a town. There is no cinema, cultural events of note are rare in the winter, and Corsican society, although outwardly friendly, can be difficult to penetrate.

A Legionnaire can apply for a marriage authorization after completing his first five years of service. Such applications are examined closely and weighed carefully before permission is granted or refused. Being a member of the *troupes d'assaut* as well as an attentive and caring husband and father can be difficult. The Legion must be practical in its decisions, guiding its men away from unwise liaisons and protecting its own interests. At the same time, it has to avoid unfeeling, bureaucratic reactions that can damage morale and end promising military careers. Such decision making tests the wisdom and human insights of the deciding officers who must be particularly alert to how the new wife might react to the demands of her new life. Once the die is cast, however, she is fully integrated into the Legion "family."

The shop at the foyer has numerous items bearing regimental identification, including sweatshirts, mugs, insignia pins, and carry-on bags. I hesitated for a moment, sorely tempted by a blue sweatshirt with the white, winged dagger of the paras and *"2ème REP"* emblazoned on it. It may have been a simple commercial product, but I knew it would be tawdry for me, as a non-Legionnaire and nonpara, to buy it or wear it.

The nearby all-weather swimming pool, the scene of various competitions, was being cleaned. I walked a short distance to the soccer field and track but a bone-chilling wind had picked up, and I did not linger very long.

The longer you stay in Corsica, the more you become aware of its winds. The *Libeccio* blows from Gibraltar to the southwest, the *Ponente* and the *Mistral* from Provence and the west, the *Tramontin* from the Po valley to the north, the *Grecale* from the Apennines to the northeast, the *Levante* from the Middle East, and the *Sirocco* from North Africa that often lays a fine dusting of ochre sand on parked cars. During a warm summer, one can live with the winds. In the winter and early spring, they can cut like a sharpened saber.

The officers and men of the 2nd REP seem to thrive on physical activity. Long before the official workday begins, the roads around Camp Raffalli and the narrow streets near the Caserne Sampiero are dotted with perspiring, jogging Legionnaires. Their activities give new meaning to the phrase "lean and mean." Common punishment for shoddy performances or minor infractions often places a Legionnaire on his stomach at any time of the day for numerous muscle-straining push-ups. Adjutant Zigic of the 3rd Company may have exaggerated a bit when he told me, "This is one of the few units in the world where the noncoms are thin," but he was close to the truth.

Even rare leisure time can be filled with weight-losing, muscle-building activities. The regiment's *Club Legion* offers its members participation in sixteen sporting activities ranging from free-fall and competitive parachuting to tennis, from judo to archery, and from wind-surfing to golf.

On my brief visit to the busy paymaster's office, I found the staff pouring over bills, requisitions, and pay records. I was shown a stack of food bills for wine, saucisson, vegetables, and fruit. Approximately 50 percent of the regiment's food is purchased from Corsican producers who have made competitive bids to provision the 2nd REP. Separate accounts cover automotive expenses: vehicles, gasoline, oil, and grease. A revolution in pay procedures during the past two years has now made it possible for a Legionnaire's pay to go directly into his own bank account. They can thus use banking cards to draw money from dispensing machines on base or from any bank in France. Legionnaires serving overseas can receive needed cash advances, while the bulk of their pay remains in trust on the base.

A stop at the camp's radio and communication section revealed that the 2nd REP had recently received the new PR4G field radios and was training operators to use them. A patient British noncom who had previously served Her Majesty for ten years attempted to explain the technicalities of the sets. Observing my puzzled expression, he simplified things. These new, secure radios scramble voice messages, allowing users to speak normally without code words. The enemy might locate the radio, but he would not be able to decipher the traffic—a considerable step forward in battlefield communications.

As is true of most technicians devoted to their craft, the noncom waxed enthusiastic about developments in his field, speaking of twenty-year advances in transmission techniques. He predicted that field telephones would soon be a thing of the past, as units will be able to use telephones with a coded card linked to a satellite.

Always a cynic when it comes to overenthusiasm for military hardware, I suggested that someone, somewhere, was probably hard at work on a scramble-breaker to neutralize the PR4G. The expert acknowledged the possibility with courtesy, but looked at me as though I had just stepped off another planet.

That afternoon I had a rendezvous with some retired paras at their *Amicale*, or clubhouse, up the hill from the *Caserne Sampiero* in the old Legion Rest Center. I was greeted by former Adjudant Fiorentini, a vital, outgoing veteran of twenty-four years in the Legion. He has served with the 1st REP in Algeria, the 1st REC (Cavalry), and the 2nd REP in Djibouti and Chad. The few former paras he could muster on short notice were introduced. After a quick tour of the neatly kept premises—office, meeting room, dining room, bar— we settled down with a cold beer to talk. These were men who had "been there and done it." They were grizzled, perhaps not so steady on their feet as previously, and full of memories. In addition to their Legion experience, these men had another thing in common—a sense of humor. Rather than bury me under a mass of war stories, they kidded each other about their Legion specialties and exchanged tongue-in-cheek comments about the "old days." Memories of dead comrades accented humorous incidents and not maudlin recollections.

"In the old Legion," Fiorentini told me, "we marched to the firing ranges. It took us all day to get there and another day to return. Now they go by truck." Another veteran spoke with a certain irony about his personal experiences with France's American allies during a joint exercise. "We were defending a beach in southern Corsica when the Marines landed. We were told to fall back but we didn't want to give up ground. We were also told to 'take it easy' and not cause trouble. A Marine butt-stroked a Legionnaire during an argument. That night two of our men, a big German and an even bigger Yugoslav, slipped out of our bivouac and went after the Marines. Two of the Americans were badly beaten."

Fiorentini remembered the North Africans who served in his company during the Algerian War with a fond smile. "They were known as "the flying carpets," he recalled. There were some discussions and misgivings concerning the large influx of eastern Europeans into the Legion. All agreed, however, that the new recruits from former Communist countries were simply following the old Legion dictum: "*La Legion est dur mais la gamelle est sûr*" ("The Legion is tough but meals are assured"). At the time of my visit, the *Amicale* was preparing for its participation in the imminent celebration of *Camerone* at Camp Raffalli and organizing the voyage of a representative to participate in *Camerone* at Aubagne headquarters.

The good-natured kidding ended when we said good-bye. They wanted me to know that they were proud of the Legion and of their past service. "One asks a lot of a Legionnaire," Fiorentini explained, "but he is always ready. A Legionnaire always does his duty."

My stay with the 2nd REP rekindled memories of *les pots dans les popotes*, or past drinks in the unit messes of Indochina. This was not always possible in wartime situations, but the French Army, and particularly the Foreign Legion, kept the tradition alive. Even supply drops to isolated outposts or long-range patrols deep in the mountainous jungles of North Vietnam could count on the inclusion of a few bottles of pastis (an old Legion remedy for dysentery), wine, or brandy. The inevitable breakage—often two bottles out of three—was enough to bring strong men close to tears.

Whether dug in on a sandstone hilltop or hunkered down overnight in a deserted village, a *coup de rouge*, a lukewarm bottle of Kronenburg beer, or a gargle of cognac helped us face the cruel realities of a seemingly endless war.

My first *pot* invitation at Camp Raffalli took me to an *Adieu des Caporaux-Chefs* for two of their comrades—a German and an Italian—both of whom had opted to leave the Legion after years of service. When I arrived shortly before noon, the beer was already flowing, and a large table was covered with snacks—pâtés and saucisson on thick bread, cheese, potato chips, and nuts.

The din in the club ceased upon the arrival of Lt. Colonel Yannick Blevin, the regiment's second-in-command, who quickly put the Legionnaires at their ease and led them in singing "Le Boudin," followed by the song of the 2nd REP. After some good-natured presentations, Blevin spoke briefly about the important role of *caporaux-chef*, describing them as "the glue that holds the Legion together." The formalities over, the colonel and his officers joined the party. My hosts saw to it that I was never without a fresh beer, while the soon-to-be-retired German told me of his plans to buy a bar in Austria that he and his wife would run together. "I will miss all this," he admitted, gesturing to his Legion comrades. His fellow retiree, the Italian, when told that my mother's maiden name had been Profumo, took to calling me "*l'Italiano*."

I spoke with *Caporal-Chef* Tran, a Vietnamese from Vung Tau, the resort town south of Saigon. We recalled the beach, the open-air restaurants, and the excellent crab served with pepper sauce and lime. Tran's father had been an ARVN (Army of the Republic of Vietnam) officer, and the family had fled during the Communist takeover. He introduced me to a husky, tatooed Laotian from Vientiane who appeared shocked upon hearing that I had returned to Vietnam in 1991. His opinion of me dropped perceptibly with I told him I had interviewed General Giap during my stay in Ho Chi Minh City. He murmured something about "Communists," made a throat-cutting gesture, and drifted off into the crowd.

A few days later, Captain Brice Houdet of the CEA invited me to another *pot* for departing members of his company. We gathered outside the barracks, as the sun dipped behind the mountains. The tables held a spread of garlic sausage, saucisson, chips, nuts, beer, pastis, wine, and—inexplicably—a bottle of John Jameson Irish Whisky. Lt. Colonel Blevin marked his appearance with a short speech and turned the proceedings over to Captain Houdet. One of the departing members of the CEA was a self-effacing Japanese *caporal-chef* whose service the captain praised. Regretting the noncom's decision to depart and return to civilian life, Houdet told him. "You'll always be welcome here, if you ever decide to return."

My ability to sniff out and attend various "*pot*" was noted by Lt. Colonel Blevin when he found me, days later and glass in hand, during a gathering in honor of some visiting Transall pilots. "You never miss a *pot*," he said, a note of wonder in his voice.

The realm of Sgt. Lance Phillips, the photographer who had gleefully suggested I jump with the CRAP team, was one of my safe havens at Camp Raffalli. Phillips and his assistant service the needs of the regiment, cover ceremonies and operations, provide official portraits and identification shots, work at maintaining current negative and print files, and find time to assist visiting writers and photojournalists. Phillips supervises all this in addition to fulfilling his normal tasks of soldiering. This includes jumpmaster assignments, marksmanship qualification, and acting as sergeant of the guard.

The photo archives provided me with a perfect refuge from the mistral winds and a good place to kill time and review my notes between appointments. It meant that I did not have to dawdle in the headquarters building with well-meaning staff officers keeping me company or suggesting fill-in activities of minor interest. Delving into these archives proved an education in itself and an important addition to my knowledge of the regiment.

Here was a wealth of visual material covering field exercises, active overseas duty and combat, ceremonies and parades, medal presentations, jump training, sports activities, and social events. A close examination of photos taken in Gabon and Rwanda provided the backdrop to the verbal and written reports on the regiment's activities in those countries during times of crisis. Scanning the color transparencies through a magnifying glass, one could almost sense the heat of the African sun, the sounds of the bush, and the ubiquitous red dust.

In March 1990, a crisis in the Republic of Gabon, formerly French Equatorial Africa, threatened the security of six thousand French citizens. When rioting occurred in Port Gentil and spread to the capital, Libreville, operation *Requin* (Shark) got underway. On May 23, the regiment's 2nd Company was put on a *Guépard* alert. The next morning word was received that the French consul and several French citizens had been taken hostage. The 2nd Company, commanded by Captain Lieutaud, flew out of Corsica for Libreville. Their task was to join with other French units in providing security and assisting in the possible evacuation of French nationals.

Upon arriving in Libreville that evening, the Legion paras secured the French ambassador's residence, protected French diplomatic and military installations, assisted in the restoration of order in the city, and ensured the liberation of hostages. On May 27, when the French government decided to evacuate French as well as foreign nationals, the 2nd Company trekked into the interior to Lamberene (the site of the late Dr. Albert Schweitzer's jungle hospital) and Rabi-Kounda in search of additional French residents.

Once the crisis had passed, the 2nd Company was cited for its many activities and for "constituting an undoubted moderating element during the return to calm of the Gabonese capital." The commander of operation *Requin* concluded, "A very fine unit, the company of Captain Lieutaud received the admiration of everyone, and above all, the honors due his regiment, the 2nd REP, in the best traditions of the Foreign Legion."

A repetition of bloody tribal clashes between Hutus and Tutsis in Rwanda in 1990 foreshadowed the large-scale ethnic massacres of 1994. After thirty years of exile in Uganda, rearmed and reorganized Tutsi tribesmen were moving on Rwanda's capital Kigali. By October 1990, the French government had decided to evacuate the 700 French nationals caught in Rwanda by the civil war. The Belgian and French governments cooperated in planning an evacuation program and maintaining the necessary security to see that it was implemented. The French called it operation *Noroit* (Northwest Wind).

Once again, the 2nd REP was the first to arrive. At 1830 on October 4, 1990, the 4th Company and the CRAP landed at Kigali airport, flown in from the staging area at Bouar in the Central African Republic. By midnight, a platoon of the company had secured the airport, while other units were in place at the French embassy and the French school.

During their first night in Kigali, the Legionnaires came under heavy fire. Snipers continued their harassment with the arrival of daylight. Captain Lemoine, now serving as security officer at Aubagne, remembers his quick trip to Kigali from Gabon.

"We went in with 138 men and a MILAN (antitank) Squad to protect the French embassy. We were mistakenly fired on by frightened Rwanda officer candidates. Despite the confusion, we managed to evacuate a group of threatened nuns. We were backed up by helicopters based in Bangui."

The arrival of additional troops, both Belgian and French, returned some normalcy to Kigali. By October 16, 1990, the 4th Company's job was finished, and it was able to leave Kigali for Bangui by road.

During the first months of 1991, three Foreign Legion Regiments—the 1st Cavalry, the 2nd Infantry, and the 6th Combat Engineers—had arrived in Saudi Arabia to join the *Division Daguet*. This division was the French contribution to the Allied forces led by Gen. Norman Schwarzkopf then preparing to oust the Iraqi Army from Kuwait. To accomplish this task thirteen NATO nations, Egypt, Syria and other Arab nations plus Czechoslovakia, Poland and Bulgaria had joined this temporary coalition. Thirty-five nations were providing manpower, armaments, or funds. Non-U.S. troop contributions numbered 200,000. The *Daguet* (yearling deer) light armored division had been placed on the left of the allied line to participate in the sweep north and to secure the western flank of the advance.

Before the beginning of the ground war, John Swain of the *London Sunday Times*, visiting the Legion positions, had noted that the Legionnaires had 30 percent more antitank weaponry in their platoons than the Americans. He saw that none of the Legionnaires wore flak jackets and was told, "We have to move faster and farther than the Americans. Flak jackets would slow us down." Swain also came away with some quotes that could come only from the Legion.

"The Legion never weeps over its dead," an officer told him. "Rather, it avenges them."

A sergeant from Manchester told Swain that "If the Legion has to fight, it will fight. The Iraqis are not that dangerous, and it is what we are trained to do."

Observing strict Muslim laws in the desert, however, was difficult. "The hardest thing is we have no red wine," another officer complained. "For us it like an Englishman without tea."

The paras of the 2nd REP had watched the departure of their comrades in the other regiments with some misgivings. True, most of the regiment had embarked on another stage of operation *Épervier* in Chad. For the majority of paras, however, to miss the desert war in the Gulf seemed a cruel blow.

They need not have worried. Plans were already under way to include the 2nd REP's CRAP team in a special grouping of parachute commandos for operations against the Iraqis. On February 9, 1991, they joined the other CRAP units of the 11th Parachute Division at Toulouse. On February 11, they landed at Riyadh in Saudi Arabia. On February 13, after receiving their reconnaissance vehicles, they moved into advance positions before Al-Rafah to await the ground offensive.

While the U.S. Special Forces and the British SAS would find themselves concentrating on the hunt for Iraqi Scud missile sites along "Scud Alley," the CRAP teams would be used primarily for special operations in support of the *Daguet* division—reconnaissance missions in enemy territory, an attack on an enemy ammunition depot, and an airmobile strike.

At 0600 on February 23, 1991, the regiment's CRAP teams moved into position for the "Desert Storm" ground offensive. By 0700 they had crossed the border into Iraq and established liaison with the 4th Company of the 2nd Legion Infantry Regiment. By nightfall they were in position to provide security for the division's advance the next morning.

At 0500, February 24, a dark, rainy morning, the *Division Daguet* broke out to the west, along with the U.S. XVIII Airborne Corps and the 82nd Airborne, to form what Gen. Colin Powell described as the "left hook" of the Allied Offensive to liberate Kuwait. The CRAP teams advanced in liaison with the 2nd Spahis until the night bivouac.

For the next three days, the division's paracommandos captured many arms and much ammunition, including heavy weapons and Kalashnikov assault rifles. Reconnaissance in helicopters and scout vehicles produced a harvest of prisoners for questioning.

These brief excerpts from the regiment's *Journal de Marche* describe daily operations:

Monday, February 25
Continued advance with the 2nd Legion Infantry Regiment; saw first Iraqi prisoners. 1500 hrs; attack on a munitions dump near d'As Salman. A Landrover flees, a number of 14.5mm weapons in working condition abandoned (by enemy). Presence of number of cluster bomb (Allied) containers. Dump securely searched. Counted several hundred cubic meters of munitions from various sources.

Tuesday, February 26

The sand storm continues. 0800 hrs, order is given for reconnaissance on the north fort of d'As-Salman. the 1st Commando (two teams from the 2nd REP plus one from the Parachute Regt. of the Marine Infantry) carry out the reconnaissance. Numerous traces of cluster bomb containers are noted. 1400 hrs, the command group is installed within the fort, forty Kalashnikov (assault rifles) and other equipment recovered. 1500 hrs: explosion of a cluster bomb, followed by a second explosion a few minutes later. Two dead and twenty-five wounded, including two from the REP's CRAP team.

Wednesday, February 27

The 2nd Team from the REP was alerted for a helicopter lift at 1300 hrs: takeoff aboard three *Puma* (choppers), and formation of a group including three *Gazelle-Hot* (missile gunships), three *Gazelle* with 20mm cannon, and one *Puma* command ship. Mission: destroy the infrastructure at d'Ash Shabaka (an Iraqi communications center). Three "Hot" missiles and one Milan missile dropped the antenna. A search of the village (by CRAP team) produced 90 Iraqi prisoners who were evacuated by helicopter. As night fell the group returned to the PC *Daguet*.

"One of our biggest problems," a team member told me, "was the large number of prisoners. We had expected more action, but the Iraqis were completely disoriented by the air strikes. Their only wish was to surrender." Other problems were the cold desert nights and freezing temperatures that often lasted into the daylight hours. Once again, the Legionnaires met their old enemy—the desert sandstorm; lashing winds that whipped their faces, sifted sand into weapons parts and engines, and lost the horizon in a yellowish haze.

The unexpected end of hostilities on February 28 came as a shock. No professional soldier seeks unnecessary risks, but there was a slight feeling of frustration among the CRAP commandos. Ordered to remain on an alert status within their sector, some paras had the feeling of a job half done. But political-military realities take precedence over what might have been. By March 8, 1991, the CRAP teams were on their way to the port of Yanbu on the Red Sea for their return to Calvi. It had been an unusually short campaign full of surprises—a campaign the 2nd REP, despite its early misgivings, had not missed.

On March 8, 1991, a headquarters group and the 4th Company of the 2nd REP were back in Rwanda, the "land of a thousand hills," for nine months. French foreign policy and its support of the Hutu-dominated government dictated the need for a strong French military presence in Rwanda for both training and security functions. This meant a recurrent presence of Legion paras, particularly in November 1991, when increased military activity by the Tutsis reactivated operation *Noroit*.

The 3rd Company had now replaced the 4th at Kigali. In December the regiment's CRAP team, actively scouting the jungle near the shores of Lake Kivu, were keeping "*Noroit*" headquarters informed of heavy fighting in the region and ensuring the evacuation of isolated French nationals.

A terse note from the 3rd Company's *Journal de Marche* paints a grim picture of the paras' daily tasks.

"Alerted for departure toward Kinyami. Following rebel actions (summary execution of nine persons including an 84-year-old nun), the Platoon escorted the French Ambassador to the site and brought the bodies back to Kigali." On March 6, 1992, the 2nd REP's contingent was relieved by another French unit and left Rwanda.

I was halfway through my stay with the 2nd REP and felt like spending an evening in Calvi away from the mess table and talk of military matters. This was no reflection on the Legion's hospitality; I merely needed some silence and time for reflection. I also wanted to explore Calvi on my own and sample some of the local cuisine. A previous trip to Corsica during the early 1960s had introduced me to *sanglier* (wild boar) served with pureed chestnuts, *merle* (blackbird) pâté, and the spicy *figatelli* sausage. I had also enjoyed the sun-kissed wine of Corsica at a Saigon bistro in 1952 and looked forward to sampling the product of the vineyards I had seen near Calvi. As I negotiated the rough cobblestones on the steep descent from the Citadel, I was not sure what the off-season restaurants might offer.

A pastis at the bar of a busy local café allowed me to observe the citizens of Calvi in a relaxed mood. The card tables along one side of the room were occupied by gravelly voiced males slapping their cards hard on the table. Loud arguments erupted, periodically punctuated by waving hands, only to subside in mumbles and shrugs. If the bistros of Paris were ignoring the new French antismoking laws, the cafés in Calvi had never considered them. The drinkers and card players were wrapped in a gray haze of smoke, and the dyed blonde behind the bar had a cigarette in the corner of her mouth as she poured my pastis. Eavesdropping was difficult as half of the customers were speaking Corsican, a Latin language with links to Tuscany and Genoa, while the others conversed in accented French.

Although the bar was on a direct line from the Citadel to the center of town, none of the Legionnaires I had seen passing by outside had decided to enter. There was no dark design to this. The Corsicans had their favorite watering holes in Calvi, while the paras had theirs—a pattern not unlike garrison towns the world over. A few days later, a Legionnaire who had seen me at the café bar warned good-naturedly that I should choose my drinking places more carefully. He said nothing against the locals, nor did he elaborate, but I sensed a certain seriousness in his seemingly jocular warning.

As I expected, many of the restaurants in town were closed. I finally selected a small, quiet restaurant off the main street that had stewed kid—a Corsican specialty—on its menu. Under a vaulted ceiling, empty tables stood covered in cloths so white they threatened snow blindness, as I was seated by the aged *patronne*. She hovered to explain the menu before going off to find a bottle of red wine from the vineyards off Calenzana.

I enjoyed a fish soup with vermicelli and croutons, dusted with grated Corsican cheese and enlivened with aioli, a rich kid stew of tender meat in a dark, spicy sauce, and a salad. The *patronne* sat at a neighboring table like a doting aunt as I ate. "Calvi is not like it was," she began ruefully, "Even the Legion has changed." My quiet, reflective evening was not to be.

8

━━◦/◦/◦━━

VIEWS OF A PROFESSIONAL

We walked into a "Mad Max" scenario at Mogadishu.

Company Adjudant Zigic,
3rd Company, 2nd REP

Media exposure of the famine and civilian suffering in Somalia during the summer of 1992 had forced the international community to react. The desperate need to end clan conflict and to provide food supplies had hastened the arrival of an international contingent, headed by the Americans, to support operation "Restore Hope." The committed troops included a strong landing force of U.S. Marines.

The paras of the 3rd Company, 2nd REP, the lead unit of the French military effort, code-named *Oryx* (Gazelle), arrived at Mogadishu airport on December 9, 1992, the day before the Marines came ashore.

"We infiltrated toward the city on foot," Adjudant Zigic recalls, "to take a strategic crossroads and control two main roads, thus securing approaches to the airport and blocking circulation of the 'technicals'".

"We walked into a 'Mad Max' scenario in Mogadishu," Zigic explained. According to him, these vehicles and their crews had to be seen to be believed. They sped through the streets and outskirts of Mogadishu like participants in some out-of-control drag race, skidding around corners on underfilled tires, scattering malnourished, slow-moving civilians before them. The gunners loosed bursts of fire into the air in warning or celebration and risked becoming airborne when their vehicles hit a bump or pothole.

The majority of "technicals" were Toyota pickups with heavy machine guns or light AA cannon mounted in the truck bed or over the cabs. Their unpredictable, heavily armed drivers were often teenagers and some of the Kalashnikov-wielding crew members were under twelve years of age. Many chewed *khat*, a stimulant drug. These irregulars were serving various clan chieftains, and some had pressured international relief organizations into hiring them to "guard" food shipments and warehouses. Their so-called security efforts were not unlike the protection rackets of the Mafia. The paras were soon aware of two prime facts regarding their Somali assignment: the local "militias" were trigger-happy, and human life had a very low priority.

The Somalis, like other peoples on the Horn of Africa, are survivors. Wiry and tough, they had experienced a long period of strict colonial rule as part of Italian East Africa before achieving independence in 1960. Their land—slightly smaller than Texas—has been plagued by droughts, deforestation, overgrazing, and desertification. Border disputes with Ethiopia and claims to Djibouti and the Somali-populated territory in Kenya and Ethiopia had contributed to considerable tension with their neighbors. Plentiful armaments and loyalty to disputatious clan leaders had helped spark continual internal unrest.

The 3rd Company's 1st platoon came under attack at its northern check point during its first night in Mogadishu and returned fire. This pattern was sustained with continued testing and harassment by militia groups. On December 14, the Legion paras were attached to a U.S. Marine battalion under the command of a Lt. Colonel O'Leary. The inland town of Baidoa, awash with starving refugees, had to be secured as a reception and distribution point for relief supplies. The Marines and Legionnaires were given the task of securing the town and its airport. Their most dangerous and delicate assignments involved the seizure of heavy weapons from renegade bands of local looters. The 3rd Company, working with Charlie Company of the Marine battalion, was supported by Marine amphibious tanks (LVTP7) during its patrol and control activities. "There was firing everywhere," Zigic recalls, "but no war."

On December 19, 1992, Zigic's platoon was on alert when he received a call from his company commander ordering Zigic and his men to join him at the American CP. There the Legionnaires participated in a joint planning conference with U.S. Marine Corps and Army officers as well as American pilots of the lethal Apache attack helicopters. The mission of this joint task force was to blow up a Somali ammunition dump, seize and disarm twenty-seven "technicals," and confiscate all available weapons. The heavily armed Apaches were to provide fire support.

When they alighted from their trucks two kilometers from their objective, Zigic and his twenty-five men were confronted by armed bands of hostile Somalis. The dangerous standoff ended when a Legion corporal fired an "intimidation round" into the ground near the feet of the menacing tribesmen. Threatened by the Legionnaires' leveled weapons and the noisy passage of ground-skimming Apaches, the Somalis reluctantly gave up their arms. The final results of the operation: the seizure of four Toyota "technicals" armed with 50-caliber machine guns; one 37mm Chinese antiaircraft gun; ten automatic rifles; twenty-one Kalashnikov assault rifles; many mines and sacks of rice (marked as relief supplies donated by France); and twenty-five prisoners captured with their arms, turned over to U.S. forces and released the next day.

On Christmas Eve, the 3rd Company's service with the U.S. Marines came to an end, and it rejoined other French units for reconnaissance and duties in and around Baidoa. The paras then celebrated a Legionnaire's Christmas in the desert. As part of the French *Batallion 13*, the 3rd Company protected food convoys, guarded depots, and provided security for operation *Oryx*, until its departure from Somalia on January 31, 1993.

Company Adjudant Zigic received the *Médaille de Valeur Militaire* and a special citation on a brigade level for his work in Somalia. Although he had not mentioned these awards during our discussion, Captain de Minieres, his company commander, told me of Zigic's decorations during a brief visit to the adjudant's office. Later, when I closed my notebook and prepared to leave, I noticed Zigic obviously had something more to say. He was direct about it. He had harsh words on the use of the Apaches' deadly firepower in heavily populated urban areas.

"The Americans massacred women and children for no reason," he said seriously, "It is irritating if a child throws a rock, but that is no reason to kill him. My first order to my men (in Somalia) was 'the first one of you who shoots a woman or child—look out.' Having witnessed the civilian casualties and tragedies caused by the use of indiscriminate firepower in Vietnam, I appreciated Zigic's candor.

During our talk, Zigic had also given me some insights into his general views on professional soldiering.

On death—"One dies once in a lifetime. I'm not interested in dying or seeing my men die. To win a war and stay alive is something not available to all."

On the importance of proper training—"It takes five years to form a soldier and only a few seconds for him to die. It takes only one bullet."

On what lies ahead—"Future wars will be fought in the cities."

On discipline—"There is no room for dialectic in the Legion. Orders are followed, and this is our great advantage."

When I left Zigic to the impatient group of 3rd Company Legionnaires waiting outside his closed door, he offered to show me Calvi by night. It was an offer I could hardly refuse, so we agreed on a tentative date and hour.

The next Saturday night, after a substantial, stomach-lining meal in the officers' mess at the *Caserne Sampiero*, I walked down the hill and along the Boulevard Wilson to the *Place de laPorteuse d'Eau* and the *Café Select*. The streets of Calvi were almost empty by 2130, the bay was calm, and there was little wind. The *Select* was advertised as a "Bar-Video-Billard" establishment, and I could hear the loud music as I approached the long, multiwindowed building.

I was a bit early for my appointment with Zigic, but that was fine, as I always like to have some time on my own to get the feel of a bar.

The *Select* was definitely "Legion country." a drinking emporium wall-to-wall with Legionnaires and their women in two large rooms. Flashing lights, blasting music, and loud conversation combined to form color and din in a basically dark environment. I elbowed my way to the bar nearest the entrance and shouted Zigic's name to a bartender. He cupped his ear, waiting for more of an effort. When I finally got through to him, he gestured toward the next room.

Standing on the threshold, I squinted into the smoky haze, trying to identify my host.

"Monsieur Simpson!" Someone shouted. "Over here!"

I walked toward the sound and found two Legionnaires I had met at the *pot* for the retiring *caporal-chefs*. The former German noncom and soon-to-be bar owner was drinking with one of his Legion compatriots. They were working their way through a bottle of Jack Daniels Black Label. They called for a clean glass and poured out a good three inches of bourbon for me.

When Adjudant Zigic arrived, I switched to Alsatian beer and—because conversation was all but impossible owing to the noise—contented myself with people watching. Most of the Legionnaires were drinking beer, and a few were sipping whisky or cognac. I recognized an officer in mufti shooting pool with some Legionnaires and was told he had come up from the ranks. The few women in the *Select* were young, sexy, and had obviously been around. Those working behind the bar appeared to have seen and heard it all before. They were quick on the riposte and not inclined to suffer indiscriminate fondling.

Sergeant Phillips arrived, surveyed the game at the pool table with interest, and promptly challenged the players to a friendly doubles game. With a wink, the German retiree told me Phillips was an "ace" with a pool cue. I waited for the sergeant to make up his duo, looking forward to seeing him triumph over his unsuspecting opponents.

I was shocked and surprised when he announced that "Monsieur Simpson" would be his partner. My honest protestations that I had not played the game for many years had little effect. Rather than enter into another "yes, you will"—"no, I won't" routine with Phillips, I accepted my fate and warned him he was bound to lose. I then asked for a quick briefing on the game. After a flicker of disbelief, the sergeant decided he would tell me what to do each time my turn came up.

Fortunately, Phillips was so skilled that he could have won the game on his own—and he did, despite my lamentable contribution. I produced a number of spectacular misses: balls hopping, skittering sideways, and smacking hard against the table's rim. When I finally did sink a long shot, and beamed with accomplishment, Phillips had to tell me I had pocketed the wrong ball.

Zigic, who was in a very quiet mood, suggested we move on to the bar *"Au Son des Guitares."* This brasserie, advertising itself as *"La Maison de Legionnaire,"* is located on a city hillside overlooking the Bay of Calvi. The long, low-ceilinged establishment was packed with Legionnaires, in and out of uniform. There were several women sitting at the bar, and I was told that some of them were non-French.

Zigic introduced me to another Legionnaire and close friend. They were soon deep in conversation, using a language I could not identify. I learned that Zigic's companion was a Croat and that they were speaking Croatian. A friendly meeting between Serbian and Croatian Legionnaires in a Corsican bar while their compatriots were ripping one another apart in the homeland must have held some lesson. Unfortunately, my mind was in neutral, I had had enough to drink, and I was beginning to glance at my watch.

I made one last attempt at sociability, striking up a conversation at the bar with two buxom Dutch women of a certain age with extreme décolletage. They had come to Corsica on an early vacation and were "enjoying Corsica without the tourists." In reality, they fit the description of the "Legionnaire hunters" to be found in abundance in Calvi during the summer months. Earlier during my stay, a Belgian *caporal-chef* had briefed me on this sociosexual phenomenon.

Beginning in June, a number of European women with a taste for macho men appear in Calvi either alone or in small groups to "have a good time." According to my informant, they range from young Scandinavian office workers to mature Italian women who have left their husbands behind in Rome or Genoa. I was told that some of the most voracious man-eaters arrive on private yachts for a week or two of priapic abandon. The *caporal-chef* had claimed the Legionnaires had to be careful not to allow the one or two weeks to extend further or to recur the following year. Most of the women understood this, he had explained, but some did not. Occasionally, this led to "difficult situations" with the women appearing unannounced in search of "their Legionnaire." How much of this was truth as opposed to fanciful conjecture was difficult to discern. But, imagining the Bay of Calvi under a full summer moon, one could entertain any number of romantic scenarios.

I finally said my "goodnights" to Zigic and his friends and climbed the dark, cobblestoned road to the Citadel. As I passed under the ancient arched gate, the group of silent, stray cats watched me resentfully as though I were intruding on their territory.

During early January 1993, the interior of a transport aircraft filled with paras of the 2nd REP was the scene of an unusual occurrence. At a given order, the paras removed their green berets and replaced them with the blue berets of a UN Protective Force. This was the first time the Legion paras had abandoned their traditional headgear for an international symbol, and not all of them were enthusiastic about the change. Shortly thereafter, the transport took off, and the Legionnaires were on their way to Bosnia-Herzegovina and the city of Sarajevo. They were flying into a city under wartime siege by the Serbs. Muslims and Serbs were at each other's throats at Bihać, Srebrenica was under Serbian shelling, and the Croats and Muslims were facing each other in a hairtrigger situation in southern Bosnia.

The regiment had profited from a hasty preparation for its participation in the UN effort in Bosnia. But the role of "peacekeepers" was not exactly tailored to the Legion's assault troops. Nevertheless, quick refresher courses on urban warfare, control, and security, and antisniper techniques helped the paras to concentrate on the problems they would soon be confronting.

Like the troops of most other involved nations, the Legionnaires were entering an unfamiliar European zone of conflict. Hardly newcomers to distant tribalism and internecine clashes, they were now about to face the ethnic and blood feuds of a disintegrated Yugoslavia in the Europe of 1993.

An advance party of the 2nd REP was already on the ground when Colonel Poulet, the regimental commander, his headquarters group, and the 4th Company, arrived in Sarajevo on January 13, 1993. Three days later, the colonel took command of the French battalion that included other French elements. By January 20, the 1st Company of the 2nd REP had joined them. This was the beginning of a prolonged and continuing French military presence in Sarajevo.

The colonel and his men were given the responsibility of defending and guaranteeing access to the besieged city's airport, an essential resupply link with the outside world. They were also to provide armed escorts for supply convoys to isolated villages and to perform humanitarian duties—such as prisoner exchanges and the evacuation of wounded civilians—in and around Sarajevo.

The paras soon learned that peacekeeping duties can be particularly hazardous. Under sporadic fire from both Bosnian Serbs and Muslims, the Legionnaires adapted to their new and trying existence. Each para had been fully briefed on situations that would allow him to return fire and carried a printed reminder to that effect. Various alert stages were established and limits placed on the approaches to the airport that would allow the French battalion to open fire once an "enemy" crossed the limit line.

Colonel Poulet had laid out definitive rules governing the various stages of alert his troops were to observe.

- Minimum intensity—helmet and bulletproof vest to be worn outside the airport zone.

- Sporadic fighting in Sarajevo or near the airport—helmet and bulletproof vest to be worn beyond living area.
- Buildup of fighting near the airport—major cutback in movements and an increase in observation. All personnel must be near radio facilities. Under maximum protection alert, all personnel are to remain in protected zones, wearing helmets and bulletproof vests. Intervention group at their post and armored personnel carrier warmed up.
- Attack on airport—activation of defense plan and orders for distribution of ammunition.

If heat and sandstorms were constant hazards in the desert, the Legionnaires in Bosnia were now facing extreme cold and heavy snow. The Legion's armored personnel carriers were sometimes immobilized by snow, and the roads became extremely dangerous under slippery ice. Para riflemen and sharpshooters guarding the airport perimeters dug defensive positions into snowdrifts and patrolled under blizzard conditions. During this period, the bombardments and bloodshed continued.

Not all the victims were soldiers of the opposing camps nor civilian residents of Sarajevo and the surrounding towns. A number of Legionnaires were wounded, and it required great restraint and discipline on the part of their comrades to remain within the guidelines of the UN rules of engagement. On February 11, 1993, Legionnaire 1st Class Ratislav Benko was killed during a mortar attack. He had just participated in the medical evacuation of a young mother and her newborn child. Pierre Dufour, a veteran of sixteen years' service in the Legion, wrote in his book *2e REP-Action Immediate* that this constant artillery harassment from the surrounding ridges reminded the paras of ". . . another sinister valley where the elite of the French Army perished. Some even went so far as to baptize the peaks that surround Sarajevo," as the French garrison had done at Dien Bien Phu.

If the possibility of direct and indirect fire was a daily threat, the consistent bully-boy tactics of the Serbs pushed the Legionnaires' patience to its limits. Despite previous agreements, there were often unjustifiable delays at Serb road blocks. Convoys carrying food and medical supplies, ambulances loaded with sick refugees, and even food supplies for UN forces had to wait on snowy roads while Bosnian Serb commanders flexed their muscles and proved how obtuse they could be. Civilian work parties sent to repair telephone lines and water supply systems under Legion escort were often held up by red tape or fired on by snipers. High-ranking French officers, insulted in front of their men, gritted their teeth and continued to negotiate according to the UN directives. Nevertheless, the Legion was learning that firmness, spiced with barely controlled anger and backed by firepower, was something the Serbs understood.

Meanwhile, the paras were perfecting techniques that would be considerably useful to other Legion and regular French Army units that would follow them to Bosnia. It was no coincidence that the 1st and 4th companies of the regiment had been among the first to arrive at Sarajevo. In addition to their expertise in antitank warfare, night action, and house-to-house fighting, the paras of the 1st were also adept as snipers. The paras of the 4th, while expert at operating behind enemy lines and demolition, were also outstanding marksmen. From the application of these specialties in a combat situation emerged practical and tested antisniper techniques. The Legion's two-man specialist teams, armed with the latest high-powered, laser-scoped rifles, were soon making it extremely uncomfortable and dangerous for the Bosnian Serb gunmen who had previously fired on Sarajevo's civilians at whim.

In May 1993, the Reconnaissance and Fire Support Company (CEA) of the 2nd REP arrived in Sarajevo to join the French battalion as reinforcements. A little over two months later, the Legionnaires of the 2nd REP left Bosnia for Calvi, shedding the blue berets of the UN for their *bérets verts*.

As of this writing, the Legion's odyssey in Bosnia continues. The pathfinder efforts of the 2nd REP have been followed by other Legion units, including the 2nd Infantry and the 1st Cavalry regiments. Most notably, the Legionnaires have been cited for their reluctance to be pushed around by any local force—Muslim, Croat, or Bosnian Serb. The role the Legion played in defense of the Franco-British artillery positions on Mount Igman, near Sarajevo, has come to the attention of the international media on several occasions.

In July 1995, as part of the new, NATO-led rapid reaction force, the Legionnaires refused to paint their vehicles UN white. A Legion sergeant, quoted in *The Washington Post*, explained, "We won't paint our vehicles UN white because that's the color of surrender." A running story from the same battle zone told of Legion snipers slipping into the forest from their bivouacs on Mount Igman to practice "aggressive protection." Col. E. D. Doyle, a military writer for *The Irish Times* of Dublin, wrote that these skilled snipers, "Lying outside the minefields," picked off "hitherto invulnerable Serb gunners (and officers) daily, using long-range Barrett (.50 caliber) sniping rifles," a tactic the Colonel described as "very unnerving."

Other stories have appeared speaking of a shadowy "special" group of Serbo-Croatian-speaking Legionnaires formed to carry the war to the Bosnian Serbs. A *London Sunday Times* report by Sam Kiley on Mount Igman had this unit, disguised as Serbs, infiltrating a Serb command post. According to Kiley, they held their daggers to the Serb commander's throat until he ordered his men to pull back from a French position. Although official French sources denied this story, they did admit such a unit had helped "break the back of the Serb field command structure by gathering intelligence behind the lines and identifying command posts."

By July 30, 1995, the same paper listed the French troops killed in Bosnia and spoke of two captains, including a doctor on a medical call, being killed by Bosnian Serb artillery fire. In the same report, a Legion "padre" was described passing out medallions of the Virgin Mary after serving communion. The padre spoke like a true Legionnaire as he warned that the medallion, "does not replace good cover and it does not replace armor. I don't do voodoo here. So be careful."

One of the most poignant photos of the Indochina War portrays a young French medical officer, wearing a parachutist's camouflage jacket, sitting in the mud of the Tonkin Delta beside the body of a dead Legionnaire. The doctor has obviously tried to save the man's life with a tourniquet, bandages, and injections, but the torn flesh was far too damaged and drained of blood to respond. The camera had caught that brief moment of despair and exhaustion before the doctor again became the professional, packed up his kit, and moved on to the next wounded man.

The medical personnel assigned to the 2nd REP today, including the young *aspirant* (officer cadet) physicians doing their temporary military service with the regiment, have something in common with that tired combat doctor in Indochina. They, too, have volunteered to treat the wounds and relieve the pain of their fellow-soldiers. To accomplish this, they must share the same operational jumps, take the same risks, and face the same enemy fire as the paras. Item 7 of the Legionnaire's Code of Honor states that a Legionnaire will never abandon his wounded or dead. This particular clause has a special meaning to the Legion's doctors. In past conflicts, they have often fallen into enemy hands or have been killed after remaining behind with the wounded and dead.

I rode to the Calvi airport one afternoon with Captain (doctor) Charrot, the young deputy commander of the 2nd REP's Medical Section. Charrot was driving an ambulance to the airport to provide a medical presence during a tactical CRAP operation. A number of commandos from the 11th Parachute Division were to drop on the field, link up with their transportation and heavy equipment, and theoretically seize the airport. The doctor and some of his team would be there to treat any human breakage.

As the unsteady ambulance bounced along the road, the captain explained that his other regular duties included daily sick call, presence at scuba diving and live-fire exercises, emergencies, and consultations by appointment for Legion families.

Charrot had previously served as a doctor with the Army Ground Forces. He had participated in operation *Daguet* during the Gulf War and later saw service at Sarajevo and Bangui. He recalled both the death of one Legionnaire in Sarajevo and the amputation he had to perform on another. He remembers most vividly the steady stream of civilian casualties—men, women, and children, passing through his battalion aid station before they were sent on to the undersupplied, understaffed, and shell-scarred civilian hospital in Sarajevo.

The 2nd REP's Medical Section team includes two supervising doctors, a dentist, a pharmacist, four experienced noncoms and fourteen medics. Each company in the regiment has a *sergent-chef* as a medical specialist. He ascertains that the Legionnaires under his care know the basic rudiments of first aid and primary treatment. Company medics carry packs with basic medical supplies including morphine. Each Legionnaire carries his own small first aid packet, including a morphine syringe that is sealed and regularly inspected.

The infirmary's ambulance crews, waiting on the edge of the Camp Raffalli DZ during a jump, are experts at breaks and sprains. Unexpected tricks of the wind, equipment tangles, bad launches, and misjudgments can all contribute to injuries, both serious and minor. The few paras I saw wearing plaster casts moving between the barracks on crutches were living proof of Newton's law of gravity.

Captain Charrot emphasized that he had few basic health problems in the 2nd REP owing to the regiment's excellent state of physical fitness. This, together with the good meals from the *ordinaire*, or mess hall, tended to make his job easier. Earlier, while waiting in the *infirmerie* for the doctor to finish with a patient, I had noted the paucity of sick call participants in his outer room. This compared favorably with the standing-room-only, sick-call crowds I recalled during training in World War II. But I did have one moment of nostalgia studying the faces of those who were waiting. Even among the hardened Legionnaires, I recognized that hurt-puppy, hang-dog look produced by a soldier about to test a doctor's patience or gullibility.

Lt. Colonel Blevin, Lt. Colonel Rideau, and Major Brottier were already at the airport, scanning the azure sky for the first sign of the "attacking" CRAP teams. Several minutes later, the commandos arrived like silent, windborne actors in one of Jean Cocteau's surrealist fantasies. Their free-fall drops had put them at some distance from the airport when their chutes opened. It was difficult to spot them against the bright sky. Navigating laterally, they rode the air currents, honing in on us, before thumping down nearby on both sides of the strip. After stowing their chutes and regrouping, the sweating commandos double-timed past us to "secure" the airport. A group of blasé baggage handlers and some construction workers hardly gave the heavily loaded, paint-smeared, special force soldiers a second look. Living side-by-side with the 2nd REP over a long period of time has accustomed the Corsicans to such antics. With the airstrip secured, a number of Transalls landed to discharge jeeps, trailers, and heavy weapons.

Once we knew the CRAP teams had landed without mishap, the captain aimed the ambulance back to Camp Raffalli. During the drive, I asked about the problem of VD and the new scourge—AIDS. I was told that when a Legionnaire got VD "in the old days" he went to jail. Now, it is treated as a strictly medical problem. The doctor explained that AIDS had thrown an "unholy fear" into the men. They now turn themselves in promptly at the first sign of any venereal infection.

We rode for a while in silence before Captain Charrot summed up his role, "A doctor must know all and keep track of everyone," he told me, "you are more a doctor than a soldier."

Our brief discussion about VD reminded me of one major change in Legion mores in my lifetime: the disappearance of the BMC, the *Bordel Militaire Contrôlé* (Controlled Military Brothel) or the *Bordel Mobile de Campagne* (Mobile Field Brothel). In peacetime, these Legion administered and controlled institutions, scattered in various locations around the world, provided a sexual safety valve for the men of isolated garrisons. They also ensured a certain degree of medical control, afforded a secure location, set prices for dallying Legionnaires, and helped alleviate tensions with the local population by slaking the ardor of passionate young soldiers.

The gritty BMCs of the North African desert were often manned by tattooed women of the Ouled Näil tribe whose predilection for fatty mutton and heavily sugared mint tea produced pneumatic, low-to-the-ground silhouettes. Legionnaires in search of younger, slimmer partners would stray to more expensive commercial establishments with attendant risks to their health and wallets. The most notorious were located in the narrow, steep alleys of the Algiers' Casbah, which wise Legionnaires only visited in strength.

During wartime, or what we now call limited intensity conflicts, the field bordellos helped ensure that no Legionnaire went into action a totally lonely man or returned from it without the feel of a woman's caress. True, these were not romantic establishments manned by slim, young houris—far from it—but they served their purpose. These were professionals in the hard sense of the term, but they were women who more than once proved the accuracy of the "heart of gold" cliché. During Vietminh attacks on French positions in Indochina, prostitutes of the BMC often tended the wounded and—in some cases—acted as litter bearers.

BMC's in Tonkin, Annam, Cochin China, Laos, and Cambodia were staffed with a heterogeneous mix of women: Vietnamese, Cambodians, Laotians, Metis, and North African, and black African professionals. Businesslike madams supervised their wards, and Legion quartermasters saw to their housing and feeding. One of the most sought-after corvées, or details, in the Legion was that of corporal of the guard at a BMC.

Not far from the sleepy Laotian capital of Vientiane in 1953, a clash between Colonial and Legion paras almost destroyed one particular BMC. The installation included three stilted Laotian huts, a makeshift "office," and a battery of generators to supply electricity. A Legion sentry guarded the BMC and a purple-nosed noncom supervised the bar in the main hut. The interior of this hut was divided into cubicles by thin walls of woven banana leaves that provided a minimum of privacy. The hut's sagging floor was made of reeds. The prostitutes were young Laotians with a propensity to giggle. If more than one cubicle were in use, the hut had a tendency to sway.

The trouble began when some paras from a Colonial Parachute Battalion began to argue over their bill. A Legion para suggested that they should try to find their own bordello rather than create problems while guests of the Legion. Push came to shove, glasses were broken, the girls shrieked, a cursing Legionnaire emerged from a cubicle securing his trousers, and the first solid blow landed with a thunk. By this time, I had retreated to a corner of the hut with my drink, trying to look as noncombative as possible. I did try to catch the sentry's attention, but he seemed rooted to his position, his back to the shouting from the unsteady hut.

A very solid head butt delivered by a large Legion para ended the skirmish. One of the Colonial paras fell heavily, there was the swishing sound of parting reeds, a cloud of dust, and the man disappeared. Everyone edged forward cautiously to peer through the newly made hole in the floor. The para lay flat on his back, bloody-nosed and unconscious, surrounded by pulverized dry reeds. The sentry, finally roused from his torpor, was attempting to awaken the casualty. The girls, relieved that the mayhem was over, were giggling nervously and picking up broken glass. Even the loser's comrades recognized the humor in the situation and agreed to a truce and an exchange of drinks.

Long after Indochina and the Algerian War, certain Legion officers vehemently defended the right of their men to *tirez un coup,* or "fire a shot" within the confines of their own BMC. Today the subject gets short shrift when outsiders are present. Sexual liberation is fine for the *citoyen,* but the thought of official bordellos for the military in this era of political correctness is enough to chill a politician's spine. Nevertheless, knowing the Legion's gift for resourcefulness, I would not be suprised to find the colored lights of a BMC blinking in the night somewhere in this world.

The regiment's 25-member deep-penetration commando team bears the unfortunate acronym CRAP (Les Commandos de Recherche et d'Action dans le Profondeur). Here a commando prepares for a mission. *BIHLE/Aubagne.*

A CRAP commando executes a HALO (high-altitude, low-opening) jump over the Bay of Calvi. *BIHLE/Aubagne.*

A commando of the 2nd REP's CRAP team with a silenced Heckler & Koch submachine gun pauses during a patrol through a palm grove during an exercise. *BIHLE/Aubagne.*

A CRAP team sniper with his scoped rifle wrapped in camouflage. *Photo by the author.*

A CRAP commando eases his heavy load prior to going into the field. He is armed with a silenced Heckler & Koch submachine gun and equipped with night-vision goggles and navigational aids. *Photo by the author.*

Capt. Bruno Schiffer (center, with wristwatch), leader of the regiment's CRAP unit, briefs helicopter pilots from the army's ground-force light-aviation detachment on his unit's special weapons and equipment. *Photo by the author.*

A visiting officer from the French Army's 11th Parachute Division (to which the 2nd REP belongs) tests the rifle of a 2nd REP sniper. *BIHLE/Aubagne.*

Para recruits learn to field-strip a light machine gun. *Photo by the author.*

The paras of the 2nd REP learn that risk, danger, and overcoming obstacles are all part of the assault course. *BIHLE/Aubagne.*

Members of a MILAN antitank missile section of the 2nd REP hump their heavy weapons up a steep hill under a hot Corsican sun. *Photo by the author.*

A sniper of the 2nd REP demonstrates his concealment capabilities. *BIHLE/Aubagne.*

Under the direction of a Japanese heavy weapons squad leader nicknamed "The Samurai," a 120mm mortar team puts their weapon into firing position high in the Corsican maquis near Calvi. *Photo by the author.*

Waiting to make a qualification jump. *Photo by the author.*

Out the rear door of a Transall transport. *BIHLE/Aubagne.*

Senior officers and noncoms present parachute wings and the regimental four-ragère of the Legion of Honor to members of the 2nd REP who have completed their jump training. *BIHLE/Aubagne.*

Companies of the 2nd REP muster at Camp Raffalli for overseas deployment. *BIHLE/Aubagne.*

The 2nd REP prepares for mobile combat patrols out of Kolwezi, Zaire, during the 1978 mission that saved the lives of hundreds of European and African hostages. *Foreign Legion.*

Col. Philippe Erulin (left), commander of the 2nd REP, confers with his officers during the Kolwezi operation. *BIHLE/Aubagne.*

Col. Bruno Dary, commander of the 2nd REP, confers with Legion and regular army parachute officers during an exercise in the Central African Republic during the 1990s. *BIHLE/Aubagne.*

Officers of the 2nd REP confer during a deep-penetration "nomadization" patrol in the Chadian desert in 1987. *BIHLE/Aubagne.*

Legion paras on the prowl for Libyan infiltrators in Chad. *BIHLE/Aubagne.*

Paras of the 2nd REP's 3rd Company confer with U.S. Marines in Somalia in February 1993. *BIHLE/Aubagne.*

Part of Operation Daguet, commandos of the 2nd REP's CRAP team pause behind Iraqi lines during the Gulf War. *BIHLE/Aubagne.*

The 2nd REP on guard at the Sarajevo airport during the Bosnian civil war.
BIHLE/Aubagne.

Chuters of the 2nd REP jump over Calvi. *BIHLE/Aubagne.*

9

THE CAÏDS

Once you've commanded in the Legion, it is difficult to adjust to another assignment. Everything else seems dull, without salt.

Lt. Colonel Yannick Blevin,
Deputy commander, 2nd REP

When the commander of a Foreign Legion unit arrives at his headquarters or encampment, the guard detachment renders honors and the bugler sounds "Au Caïd." As a Caïd is an Arab chieftain, the modern Legion once again harkens back to its historic roots in the desert. Many of the Legion's Caïds have been legendary. From the suntanned, rough officers who led their men through the conquest of Algeria during the early 1800s, to the slender, mustachioed and goateed Captain Danjou, who died at Camerone hacienda in 1863 and left his wooden hand as a symbol of sacrifice; from the bearded, bemedalled General Paul Rollet, the "father of the Legion," who nurtured and protected the Legion through difficult times in the 1930s, to Lt. Colonel Jules Gaucher, commander of the famous 13th demi-brigade, who died in the first Vietminh artillery barrage at Dien Bien Phu in 1954.

Lt. Col. Gaucher—with whom I shared a bottle of Scotch at Dien Bien Phu—was a perfect example of a contemporary Caïd. The forty-eight-year-old graduate of Saint Cyr, who had served in Indochina since 1940, was tall, tough, and irascible but respected by his men who referred to him as "*le vieux* (the old man)." Gaucher had led his Legionnaires on operations throughout Tonkin. They had fought the Japanese, the Vietminh, a marauding force of Chinese nationalists, and bands of tribal pirates. Lt. Colonel Gaucher had been no stranger to Dien Bien Phu, having carried out a delaying action against the Japanese there in 1945 before leading his Legionnaires to safety over the Chinese border. The hard-drinking colonel and his staff, a sort of Legion "mafia," had an equally bellicose reputation for fistfights in the bars

119

and dance halls of Hanoi and Saigon during their rare absence from the field. Because of his long service in Southeast Asia, Gaucher might more appropriately be titled a warlord or mandarin, but he was, indeed, a true Caïd in the Legion tradition.

Today's Caïds may seem a bit more subdued than their colorful predecessors, but they are just as hard and professional. One trait that has not changed is the volume of their voices. Like most combat leaders, Legion officers are shouters. Bellowing instructions on the firing range, shouting the location of a DZ over the throbbing engines of a Transall, comparing notes on a coastal map as a Zodiac bounces toward shore, making your orders clear in the face of a Tramontane wind, or chewing out a Legionnaire whose weapon needs cleaning, requires mature lung power. MLP is not easily acquired. It comes with the day-to-day demands and trials of a troop commander. The miracle is that the volume can be lowered to suit a different environment. A veritable roaring tiger in the field or office can appear at a social evening and speak in calm, normal tones.

Col. Bruno Dary, the forty-two-year-old commander of the 2nd REP, was in the Central African Republic with units of the regiment during my visit to Camp Raffalli, but a brief review of his career provides an insight into the background of someone who commands the only Parachute Regiment of the Foreign Legion.

After his graduation from Saint Cyr as a lieutenant, Colonel Dary went directly to Corsica and the 2nd REP for a four-year assignment as a platoon commander. This included participation in the Kolwezi operation under Colonel Erulin. Subsequent assignments took him to French Polynesia, to Castelnaudary where, as a captain, he headed the company for Cadre Instruction, to the headquarters of the 11th Parachute Division for four years as a specialist in the techniques of airborne operations. During this period, he prepared the entrance examination for the *École de Guerre* and followed courses at the Faculty of Toulouse. After two years at *l'École Supérieure de Guerre*, he returned to the Foreign Legion for a two-year assignment with the 13th demi-brigade at Djibouti. On his return to France, he was assigned to the General Staff Headquarters in Paris where he specialized in the commitment of forces for overseas operations. His subsequent appointment as commander of the 2nd REP in 1994 witnessed his return to the regiment he had joined as a young lieutenant eighteen years previously. Married and the father of five children, Colonel Dary is a qualified parachute and commando instructor. A graduate engineer, he holds a degree in political science, and the diploma of higher military studies. He is a Chevalier of the Legion of Honor and holds the Cross of Military Valor.

Lt. Colonel Blevin, Colonel Dary's deputy, received me in his sunlit office in the early afternoon. He was speaking in a calm, normal voice, but he had a raw bruise on his nose received during a morning jump with his men. A forty-five-year-old graduate of Saint Cyr, Blevin joined the 2nd REP for the first time in 1979 after serving with a regular army infantry regiment. Other assignments took him to French Polynesia for a year with the Legion's 5th Regiment; to Chad where he commanded the 2nd REP's 4th Company during operation *Manta* from November 1983 to April 1984; to a staff assignment in Paris; to the Legion's 2nd Infantry Regiment at Nîmes and participation in operation *Requin* (shark) in Gabon during 1990. He joined the Joint Headquarters of French Armed Forces, Southern Zone, Indian Ocean in 1992, before being assigned to his present post.

A Chevalier of the Legion of Honor and recipient of the Cross of Military Valor, Lt. Colonel Blevin is a qualified commando instructor and a graduate of the General Staff School. He is also married, the father of three children, and—as acting commander of the regiment—very busy. He is a tall, large-framed man who does not waste words. The interview was interrupted by phone calls, urgent signatures, and rapid consultations through a partially opened door. He obviously wanted me to understand his feelings for the Legion and particularly the relations between the Legion's officers, noncoms, and men.

"Once you've commanded in the Foreign Legion," Blevin explained, "it is difficult to adjust to another assignment. Everything seems dull, without salt. You are always proud to be a Legionnaire." He explained that, despite "rigid" discipline, relations between the ranks and the officers remain close. "If a Legionnaire insists on seeing his captain or even his *chef de corps* (unit commander), he cannot be refused. This is the frankness that makes the Legion." He talked of the continual informal discussions or chats with his men, "even during the changing of the guard." I might have been skeptical of this assertion, if I had not seen Blevin a few days earlier talking and laughing with his guard detachment following its formal presentation. I had also observed him, completely relaxed, mixing with his noncoms and men during various "pots" at Camp Raffalli. He made a special point of telling me that he knew all the regiment's noncoms personally. But Blevin did not give me the impression of being a social creature. Riding to and from the Citadel at mealtimes, we seldom made small talk, and I noted a certain introspection on his part—introspection that comes with responsibility.

Our interview was interrupted again. This time it was the sous-préfet, the senior regional representative of the French government. I offered to leave, but Blevin gestured for me to remain. The préfet was calling to thank Blevin and the 2nd REP for assistance rendered during a recent prime ministerial visit to Corsica. He also expressed his appreciation for being informed in a timely manner of the details concerning the Transall crash in the mountains.

Blevin rang off by reassuring the préfet that the regiment was always ready to help in any circumstances.

We then discussed recruiting and the problem of ascertaining that new volunteers fulfilled their enlistment contract. Blevin considered any premature departure from the ranks—either legal or by desertion—as a failure. He said that the regiment made a special effort to assimilate the newcomers, but individuals who fail to acclimate might be permitted to depart within six months of their enlistment. But, he explained, the majority remain and are held together by the Legion's traditions, camaraderie, and the pride that comes from being a member of a famous corps.

Blevin recalled his first departure for Chad when he was commander of the 4th Company. A Libyan incursion into Chad had been reported, and he had been called into the office of the regimental commander, Colonel Janvier, on Sunday morning, August 15, 1983. Under a *Guépard* alert, two companies, including the 4th, were to leave for Chad immediately. "By 2300 hours that night," Blevin said with obvious pride, "both companies were rallied and ready."

I mentioned the few faded "*Legion Fourra*" ("Legion Out") graffiti I had noticed on some walls in Calvi, the equivalent of the "Yankee Go Home" messages popular in France during the formation of NATO in 1949. Blevin shrugged them off as inevitable given the present political climate in Corsica. He described the regiment's local relations as "good but not great" and pointed out that the improving Legion–civilian contacts was very much on the regiment's agenda.

He was telling me about a sergent-chef he had had in his 4th Company who had been a general in the Croatian Army, when we were interrupted by a solid knock at the door. A captain reminded Blevin that he had an appointment elsewhere, which ended our interview.

Later, relaxing in the sun near the momentarily peaceful DZ, I pondered the mix of traditions that hold the Legion together. I decided that much of it is based on the proposition that everything about the Legion is unique. The Legion has both its own distinct uniform and headgear and its own green and red flag, inherited from the Swiss of the 2nd Legion serving France in 1885. The Legion's combat engineers wear a distinctive regulation beard. The Legion has its own band of one hundred musicians that differs from other French military bands by the use of fifes, and the carrying of a burnished pole topped by a shining metal "chapeau chinois" (chinese hat) decorated with tiny bells and two horsetail plumes. The latter, according to Arab tradition, represent the tails from the mounts of defeated enemies. Finally, unlike other French Army units, the band's snare drums are worn low on the drummer's leg.

The Legion marches to a slow cadence of 88 strides a minute compared with the standard infantry cadence of 120 strides a minute. "Le Boudin," the Legion's marching song, named after the sausage roll of tenting carried on a Legionnaire's pack many years ago, is sung to the same slow rhythm as the marching cadence. These seemingly small distinctions combine to proclaim "we are different."

I reflected on the unique ceremony of the *képi blanc*. The torchlit ceremony takes place at sunset. After the commanding officer reminds the young Legionnaires that they have sworn their honor and loyalty to the Legion, all present join in singing "Le Boudin," and the recruits don their prized *képi blanc*.

The importance of the *képi blanc* as a Legion symbol was recently underscored in the French film "Dien Bien Phu" by director and member of the French Academy Pierre Schoendoerffer, himself a Dien Bien Phu survivor. A moving sequence based on an actual occurrence just before the fall of the French mountain stronghold depicts a mud-smeared Legionnaire removing his helmet and replacing it with a *képi blanc*. When his officer questions this action, he explains, "I want them (the Vietminh) to know they are facing the Legion."

Equally important to the assimilation process are the various fêtes, or celebrations, that combine to bring the Legion "family" together. Christmas Eve, or Réveillon, at Camp Raffalli and other Legion posts is a special event, particularly for unmarried Legionnaires and those without a home. Traditionally, all the officers and noncoms remain with their men for this celebration. It includes a midnight Mass followed by a special dinner, a distribution of gifts by the company commander, a contest to choose the best crèche, or manger scene, the presentation of humorous satirical "sketches" that often cut close to the bone, and the toasting of Noël into the early hours. Outsiders may find such celebrations incongruous considering the multiethnic, multireligious composition of the Legion. Nonetheless such echoes of France's historically Christian armed forces appear to pose no problem for today's Legionnaires regardless of their beliefs.

On January 1, the noncommissioned officers present their best wishes to the officers and invite them to their mess or *popote*. On January 6, Epiphany, known in France as "*la Fête des Rois*," the officers play host to the noncommissioned officers. The bean hidden in the "Cake of the Kings" is "found" by a preselected recipient, usually a worthy noncom, who becomes king for a day. This distinction entails delivering a ribald speech, organizing his court, and promulgating numerous humorous ordinances. He later visits the mess kitchen for a bit of royal soup tasting. The *Chef de Corps*, or unit commander, remains at the "king's" side as an adviser throughout his short reign. Although these traditional events may have found their origin in the need to obviate boredom in faraway posts, they continue to bring Legionnaires of all ranks together, emphasize their interdependence, and strengthen the bonds of camaraderie.

My next appointment was with Lt. Colonel Rideau, the regiment's operations officer, a wiry, bespectacled Saint Cyr graduate who first served with the 2nd REP from 1980 to 1987. He interrupted his planning duties to brief me on his responsibilities. Rising from a desk piled with paperwork, he stood looking out the window while he listed the companies that were currently overseas. The 1st was in Bouar, Central African Republic, the 2nd was stationed in the republic's capital of Bangui, and the 4th was in Libreville, Gabon. Normally, he explained, the companies change assignments every four months. This system of rotation provided the Legionnaires with experience and familiarized them with specific areas where they may be called upon to serve.

Rideau, a calm, good-natured officer, had passed through the *École de Guerre* and the General Staff school before spending two years in French Guiana from 1992. He explained that, although the regiment must maintain its viability as a parachute-infantry unit, it was orienting itself toward more special operations and commando-type activities, including "the capability to do things differently," for example, to "strike with hammer blow force." This would mean continued development of the company specializations, a concentration on the physical, intellectual, and psychological potential of the regiment's personnel, and maintaining the *esprit para* that, in itself, guaranteed efficiency. Rideau explained that the 2nd REP had no trouble finding officers of high quality as the six companies had slots for only six captains and twenty-five lieutenants. Candidates had "to fight" for a place.

Although many of the Legion's officers are Saint Cyr graduates or products of other military schools, there are still those rare individuals who have come up through the ranks. Maj. Maurice Cote, whom I met at Aubagne, joined the Legion at the age of eighteen, signing up as a citizen of Monaco. He described today's Legion as "less simple" than the organization he had joined as a young man. Cote went into action with the 2nd REP at Kolwezi and later in Chad. He made corporal in 1968, sergeant in 1969, adjudant-chef in 1973, and passed through the officer's training school to become 2nd lieutenant in 1979. In 1980 he became a 1st lieutenant, a captain in 1984, and a major (commandant) in 1992. This success story is tempered by Cote's revelation that, "When I was working my way up the ladder, three or four enlisted men became officers annually. In 1994, only two were commissioned."

Maj. Gen. Christian Piquemal, the present commander of the Foreign Legion, is the ultimate Caïd. This tall, athletic soldier of fifty-seven began his career with the 2nd REP and wears his parachute wings with obvious pride. An officer who has distinguished himself in advanced military studies, including time as a professor at the *École Supérieure de Guerre,* and a recipient of a degree in atomic engineering, General Piquemal's eyes light up when he recalls his days as a para. Despite his hectic schedule visiting Legion units throughout the world, he found time to answer some of my questions about the 2nd REP and the Foreign Legion in general.

Q. When were you assigned to the Legion, in what capacity, and what were your first impressions?

A. I served in the Foreign Legion for the first time as a 2nd Lieutenant when I graduated from the Infantry School on August 1, 1963. At that time, I was assigned to the Training Group of the Foreign Legion at Bonifacio, Corsica, as a platoon commander of volunteer recruits.

I was intimidated, fascinated, and proud, all at the same time. Intimidated to have to command such unusual men. Fascinated to be in that Legion that had filled my imagination since adolescence by its mysteries, myths, and reputation. Proud to belong to a prestigious elite corps.

Q. What changes have you noted in the Legion since your first assignment?

A. In one sense, the Foreign Legion has not changed in thirty years. Its foundation rests on four pillars: the nature of its mission, the rigor of its execution, its solidarity, and the cult of remembrance. After 164 years, they are the essence of the Legionnaire's ethics, and they remain unchanged. Only [the Legion's] recruitment, reflecting political, economic, and social crises, the organization, and the location have changed. Essentially European during the 1960s [western and central Europe], recruitment has become worldwide in the 1980s. Since 1990, its composition includes a majority of candidates from former Warsaw Pact nations. Located in North Africa until 1962, between 1963 and 1974 the Foreign Legion was redeployed to France (six regiments) and throughout the world, where it has shown its excellent adaptability.

Q. When, and for how long, did you serve with the 2nd REP? Why did you volunteer for jump training as a para?

A. I served in the 2nd REP for five years, from August 1, 1964, to August 31, 1969, as platoon commander, sports officer, and second in command of a company. Since my youth, I had it in my head to be a parachute officer. I passed my premilitary qualification as a parachutist at the age of eighteen when I was in high school. Then I obtained my military jump qualification in 1961 at the military academy at Saint-Cyr Coetquidan. On joining the Legion, it was only natural that I decided to serve with the 2nd REP, the sole heir of the Legion's parachute regiments.

Q. With which companies did you serve in the 2nd REP? What overseas postings did you have?

A. I served successively with the 1st Company, the 3rd Company, and the Company of Support and Reconnaissance (CEA) at Bou-Sfer, Algeria, from 1964 to 1967 as platoon commander and sports officer. Finally, I joined the 4th Company at Calvi from 1967 to 1969 as chief of the advanced training group and deputy commander. Overseas assignments included three years in Algeria, and eight months in New Caledonia. I spent six months a year in French Polynesia from 1976 to 1980 and two years in French Guiana from 1985 to 1987.

Q. When did you leave the 2nd REP, and with what other Legion units have you served?

A. I left the 2nd REP in 1969. I then completed a course of Higher Military Studies, served in the Chasseurs Parachutistes and at the French Nuclear Experimentation Center. I returned to the Legion as second in command of the 4th Regiment at Castelnaudary from 1980 to 1982. From 1985 to 1987, I commanded the 3rd Legion Infantry Regiment at Kourou, Guiana.

Q. How would you rate the 2nd REP in comparison with other parachute assault units, both French and foreign?

A. The 2nd REP is an exceptional regiment in the proper sense of the term: both Legionnaire and parachutist. It's a regiment ready at all times for unusual and difficult missions. In fact, it's the only regiment in France stationed on an island and benefiting from a unique setting for its training—Corsica. With seven basic, specialized units, it possesses remarkable flexibility for all its missions. It can draw on an exceptional human potential both in quality and quantity (1,350 men of 70 nationalities). It carries out advanced technical training, notably in the science of airdrops and air delivery. In sum, the 2nd REP considers itself the spearhead regiment of the Foreign Legion, faithful to its motto "*More Majorum,*" or "In the Steps of Our Predecessors."

Q. Have you participated in joint operations with foreign units? Can you describe such experiences, particularly in regard to American units—Airborne or Marines?

A. Periods of training with foreign units are rare, but we can cite the regular participation of the 2nd REP with the U.S. Marines in southern Corsica during exercise *Fregate*. Above all, I want to emphasize that during Operation *Restore Hope* in Somalia, the 3rd Company (2nd REP) commanded by Captain Mercury impressed more than one Marine!

Q. What is the importance of discipline in today's Legion?

A. Discipline remains essential because it is the army's main strength, but it is even more so when it comes from the intelligence of the heart, when it is freely accepted.

Q. Critics of the Legion often use the terms *archaic* and *mercenary* in their attacks. What is your response?

A. *Archaic* and *mercenary*—I'm ready to supply a dictionary to our detractors so they can learn the meaning of those terms.

My response is clear:

The Legion doesn't belong to the past. On the contrary, it is now, more than ever, effective and required. Engaged in every theater where France is present, having at its command qualified personnel trained for all missions, using the latest equipment, it can respond to any unforeseen intervention without requiring the authorization of parliament and without creating a public dispute. Is that being archaic?

The Foreign Legion is an integral part of the Army Ground Forces. It obeys the same rules and regulations, fulfills the same missions, possesses the same structures, but differs only by the unique statute of the Legionnaire. In addition, the Legionnaire doesn't receive special pay, or conduct special wars. Therefore, the Foreign Legion possesses none of the characteristics of a troop of mercenaries. Last point, and not the least important: we accept one Legionnaire for every seven who volunteer.

Q. The Foreign Legion has always been known for its adaptability to new requirements and its ability to survive. How do you see the future of the Legion in a rapidly changing world?

A. The Foreign Legion has now existed for almost 165 years. It's in good health and appreciated and valued by the highest civilian and military authorities of the state. Its remarkable image testifies to the consideration and esteem it enjoys. It's a modern force, efficient, immediately available, an indispensable tool for the French government.

Whatever changes there are in armies, the Legion will without doubt maintain a privileged and envied place within the military institution. I don't believe its future is threatened. Certainly, its future will be decided by France. But I'm not uneasy because—since the Algerian war—the Legion has shown its extraordinary capacity to adapt and its efficiency in the most difficult and varied missions it has had to accomplish.

Whatever the Legion's future, there is little doubt that its members are well fed. At noon on a Monday at Camp Raffalli, a day like any other, the hungry paras of the 2nd REP sat down to the following menu:

Onion Tart
Roast Pork with Prunes
Parsleyed Cauliflower
Salad & Cheese
Fruit Yogurt

Their dinner that night featured watercress soup, grilled chicken thighs, noodles with mushrooms, green salad, and fresh fruit. These meals were accompanied by freshly baked bread and a choice of wine, beer, or soft drinks. Other main dishes from the week's menus included roast leg of lamb, pork chops, stuffed veal, sea trout, steak, and roast chicken with tarragon.

Forty-three years earlier, in the wartime press camp of the French Army in Hanoi, an Information Officer had stamped my *ordre de mission* with a flourish and offered some advice. "When you're in the field," he had said, "try to eat with the Legion." As a neophyte to Indochina and an official war correspondent of the U.S. Information Service, I had taken his advice with a grain of salt. After all, I had reasoned, I was there to cover the growing pains and hopeful "triumphs" of the new Vietnamese National Army, not the daily travails of the French Expeditionary Force.

It was soon obvious, however, that the Information Officer had spoken the truth. True, I was observing the shaky birth of the VNA (later the ARVN) at first hand, but the "triumphs" were few and far between. Meanwhile, although I had developed a taste for Vietnamese food and the ubiquitous nuoc mam sauce, the raw products the Vietnamese "beps" (cooks) had to work with in the field did not equal those found in the better Vietnamese restaurants of Saigon and Hanoi. It was also true that my uninitiated western stomach was not ready for the cursory sanitation methods of Vietnamese field kitchens. These included washing shared bowls and chopsticks in murky water from the rice paddies and indiscriminate hawking and spitting by the mess personnel.

It was not long before I was tempering my Rooseveltian views of colonialism and pushing my jeep that extra mile or taking a detour in search of a more compatible diet. North African units, noted for their cous-cous, chorba soup, or occasional méchoui of lamb roasted on a spit, were a sometime target. But arrival at a Legion CP on or about mealtime was a cherished goal, come mud, mines, or the threat of ambush.

One memorable meal shared with the Legion in Tonkin Delta during the winter of 1953 was typical of such culinary interludes. I had rolled to a muddy stop inside the barbed wire of a fortified post. The tricolor and the red and green banner of the Legion snapped overhead in the cold wind. The 105mm howitzers of a Colonial artillery battery were coughing out a harassing fire and dropping empty brass shell casings clanking onto a growing pile.

Forewarned, my Legion hosts greeted me with a glass of pastis and introductions were made. After another jolt of Marseille throat opener, we moved to a makeshift table within the CP. Once seated, a young officer read the menu. The first course paid tribute to our location: a soupe Tonkinoise, or Pho, of rich beef broth, rice noodles, scallions, and strips of beef flavored with fresh coriander. The main course, filet de boeuf Perigourdine, was a masterpiece of improvisation. Thinly sliced water buffalo meat substituted for beef filet and black Chinese mushrooms replaced the truffles in a rich, dark sauce that lapped the edges of our pommes mousseline. A plentiful supply of wine from Mâcon helped the buffalo go down.

Let me pause to explain the French Army's tradition of wine-quaffing. Since the Gauls carried off the first captured Roman amphoras brimming with wine, to the full carafes on the mess tables of the Maginot Line in 1939, to the ceremonial toasts of today drunk at the commanding officer's table, wine has been an integral part of French military culture. More an addition to nourishment than an adjunct to drunkenness, the *gros rouge* that accompanies a

Legionnaire's meal is considered his due and the needed addition for the full enjoyment of his meal. The uninitiated or unapproving might be surprised to find how few troopers overindulge. They would also be surprised to observe—on a cold day—how little deleterious effect a drop of cognac in the morning coffee might have.

A salad of bean sprouts, onions, and Belgian endive (pilfered from the headquarters mess at Nam Dinh) cleared our palates for a syrupy egg flan prepared by a former pastry chef. Strong coffee, Cognac or Mirabelle were served to accompany the standup toasts to the United States, France, the Legion, and the ranking chef. Somehow, after a meal with the Legion, the wartime Tonkinese landscape did not look so menacing, and the future had a softer edge.

Since Indochina, I have shared food with a number of military units. The Royal Marine Commandos have a certain touch with tinned beef, beans, and ketchup. The members of Britain's Parachute Regiment seem to believe a packet of curry powder can improve any rations. I have picked sand out of my teeth at a U.S. Navy clambake in Rhode Island, breakfasted on soaplike cheese and pickled herring with Norwegian infantry during a NATO exercise, and gobbled hunks of black (blood) pudding following a talk to an audience of Irish reservists in Cork. But nothing has quite equaled the food and ambiance at a Legion table.

During the late 1980s, I spent some time with the Legion's 4th (training) Regiment at Castelnaudary where the new trainees were burning up a huge number of daily calories and learning the meaning of true fatigue. A typical lunch at "Castel" included a first course of sliced salami (*saucisson*), ham, and garlic sausage with a salad of shredded raw carrots, tomatoes, green peppers, and lettuce. The main course was stuffed veal with buttered noodles, and a last course offered cheese. That evening, the meal began with leek and potato soup, followed by a bacon omelette with mashed potatoes and ended with fruit and cheese.

The warrant officer in charge of the cuisine at Castelnaudary had told me that second helpings were acceptable but third helpings were frowned upon. The Legion, he explained, had become weight conscious. Surveying the long tables, I noted the strategically placed, crisp loaves of freshly baked bread, but the clusters of wine bottles I remembered from the past were missing. I was told that wine was available, but most of the younger Legionnaires now preferred cola or orange and lemon drinks, particularly at midday. I was further disillusioned when the warrant officer told me the trainees' favorite meal was now *steak haché, pommes frites* with plenty of *sauce tomate,* or hamburger steak with fried potatoes, doused with ketchup. An invitation to the *caporal-chef's* mess restored my morale. Pastis was flowing at the bar and bottles of Côte du

Rhône emblazoned with the mess insignia were available at the tables. When a husky *caporal-chef* with tattooed forearms welcomed me to the table and filled my wine glass, I was reassured to find that the young soft drink enthusiasts in the other mess had not imposed their preferences on the old breed.

So it was that I approached my rendezvous with the top chef of the 2nd REP with enthusiasm. I had encountered *Sergent-Chef* Pastrovicchio briefly when arranging our meeting, and he appeared both cooperative and jovial. More important, he had the reassuring silhouette of someone who enjoyed the fruits of his labor. Despite his rotundity, Pastrovicchio is still an active jumper and—like all Legionnaires—a combat soldier. He had served as a chef in Sarajevo, keeping the paras fed under difficult conditions.

Although I had asked to observe the simple day-to-day operation of the kitchen, I was greeted with a glass of champagne and canapés. Pastrovicchio introduced me to his staff, including a smiling, dark-skinned assistant from Pondicherry (formerly French India) a husky Japanese, an English noncom who handled the mess accounts, a German, and a New Zealander. I asked the apprentice Japanese chef if he had ever prepared a Japanese dish for his colleagues.

"I was never a cook in Japan," he replied, seriously. "I am just learning to prepare French food." I had the impression this particular "samurai" still thought food preparation was women's work. Pastrovicchio then proceeded to brief me on his domain. The busy kitchen produces one hundred forty thousand meals a year featuring fresh products from Corsica and the French mainland. Since taking over the mess the *sergent-chef* has pooled chefs, revamped the existing provisions procedures, and is supervising the installation of new kitchens—the first in forty years. At the time of my visit, he had begun a training program for the chefs from the combat companies, each of whom were to spend four weeks working in the central kitchens.

Pastrovicchio and his assistants identified the two favorite dishes of the Legion paras. They relish that classic of French bourgeois cuisine, *blanquette de veau* (veal stew with a sauce of stock, egg yolks, and cream); and cous-cous, the North African blend of semolina grain, lamb or chicken, spicy sausages, and chick peas moistened with a rich broth livened with piquant *harissa* sauce. These favorites appear regularly, but the weekly menu is based primarily on what the paras need as a sound diet as well as what they prefer to eat.

I was shown the Legion's combat ration packets. The warm menus include: mushroom, tomato, and leek and potato soup; mutton with beans; chicken curry; pork with lentils; and a cassoulet. In addition to instant coffee and a chocolate drink, the paras can indulge their desire for sweets and replace energy with bars and packets of nougat, caramels, fruit bars, and bonbons. Although the French Academy, that guardian of the French language and enemy of Anglo-speak, might not approve, the ration contents also list "chewing-gum." Liver pâté, tuna in oil, mackerel with mustard sauce, and tinned beef figure among the cold choices to be eaten when cooking or heating is impossible. During the Gulf War, the Legionnaires often traded their rations for American cigarettes or other items from U.S. soldiers and marines who had grown weary of their own uninspired "Meals Ready to Eat."

We sat down to a lunch of varied hors-d'oeuvres, followed by roast chicken and potatoes, salad, and cheese, an ice cream dessert, and coffee. We drank the Côte du Rhône from the Legion's vineyards at Puyloubier. It was an enjoyable, if not leisurely, lunch. Legionnaires have healthy appetites and are accustomed to a tight schedule. Upon cleaning their plates with alacrity, they must then wait patiently for a guest to catch up before the next course appears. As a slow eater, busy asking and answering questions, I continually found myself lagging behind at the table. Under the scrutiny of hungry paras with a busy afternoon ahead of them, I often solved the problem by leaving a course unfinished.

Every mess kitchen is incomplete without an in-house character. The 2nd REP has Antoine, an overweight, aged Corsican with few teeth who drives his mule and cart to the Camp Raffalli mess each day to pick up refuse for his pig farm. Along the way, he responds to the honks of the horn and waves from the sedans of para officers and enlisted men's jeeps, acknowledging these greetings as his due. Antoine has known every regimental commander since the 2nd REP arrived in Calvi. A place is reserved for him at the head chef's table where he lights into the food and wine with gusto. Rumor has it that Antoine, the pig-slop man, owns a great deal of land and much highly desirable property in and around Calvi. He appeared to find my presence at Pastrovicchio's table a great source of amusement. Raising his wine glass in my direction more than once, he emptied it in a silent toast, thus requiring an immediate refill. I could not help wondering whether a young Antoine might not have wolfed down pancakes and bacon courtesy of the USAAF in 1944 when Fiume Secco was a base for American B-17s.

At the end of the meal, I was presented with a choice bottle of Legion wine and told I was always welcome to return. I thanked Sergent Chef Pastrovicchio profusely, shook hands all round, and left the chefs to their work. Later, being driven back to the Caserne Sampiero, I saw Antoine and his loaded cart heading slowly back toward Calvi behind his plodding mule. He acknowledged my wave with a grin and a nod of his head. As a newcomer, I did not yet qualify for a responsive wave.

There are three officers' messes at the Caserne Sampiero: a Senior Officer's mess, a Captain's mess, and a Lieutenant's mess. Each has its own protocol and traditions. A wide stone stairway leading to the top-floor bar is hung with the insignia from French and foreign units who have visited the regiment. Officers of all ranks gather before the long, high bar about noon to munch peanuts and other snacks with their drinks. Much beer, some tomato juice, and a few glasses of pastis are in evidence. In good weather, some officers take their drinks out onto the wide, sunbaked roof terrace that overlooks the Bay of Calvi. The high-ceilinged bar is decorated with Legion memorabilia and trophies from various overseas assignments. Africa is well represented by spears, swords, and paintings. There is a large brace of old Lebel rifles with fixed bayonets on one wall and a brace of bayoneted French carbines on another.

The officers of all ranks socialize until the arrival of the colonel at approximately 1230. A strident call to attention signals the arrival of the commanding officer and his deputy who join the group for a quick drink before heading for the Senior Officer's mess on the same floor. The captains and lieutenants then peel off, clattering down the stairs to their separate messes. Each mess had its own special atmosphere but all follow the same specific rules:

- No rising from the table without authorization.
- No eating until the mess president commences.
- No service business at table.
- No war stories (*raconter ses campagnes*) at table.

The senior officer's mess is comparatively quiet and reserved. Discussions can range from local politics to the cinema. During my numerous meals with the senior officers, I was asked some questions about U.S. foreign policy. Such queries were difficult enough when I was still in harness as a Foreign Service officer with access to briefing papers and classified material. Now, with light years between myself and the slow-grinding bureaucracy of Washington, I find that my answers are primarily personal opinions buttressed by avid reading of the International Herald Tribune. I do not think my interlocutors were impressed. After meals, upon moving to a low table for coffee and a digestif, the rules no longer applied, and we were able to discuss items three and four without restriction.

The captain's mess is one floor lower. Many of the youthful captains are company commanders. They are considerably more boisterous than the majors and colonels above them. During my stay at Calvi, the *popotier* of the captain's mess was an officer from the 1st Legion Cavalry Regiment on temporary duty with the 2nd REP. As *popotier* his duty was to ensure the smooth operation of the mess, which he achieved to everyone's satisfaction. His greatest test came when he was called upon to open two bottles of champagne in the cavalry manner with a desert sabre to celebrate the birthday of a mess member. He did it neatly and with panache without losing more than a few drops. This performance earned him a grudging round of applause, and we toasted the birthday with enthusiasm. Then it was time for the captains to leave the Citadel, find their jeeps, and speed back to their companies at Camp Raffalli.

A bit farther down the ancient steps is the lieutenant's mess, a constant circus of youthful high spirits, a cross between a fraternity party and an unruly bun fight. The president of this mess rules over the table with an iron hand, levying penalties for offenses, real or imagined. A lieutenant wishing to drink a glass of wine must ask permission. When the president grants the request, the officer drinks down the full glass and states, "The wine is excellent, *Monsieur le président.*"

The president can pose questions to any officer at the table. If the officer answers incorrectly, inadequately, or his attitude displeases the president, he can be escorted by the *popotier* to the "prison," a nearby room with a heavy, bolted door. If the *popotier* fails to bolt the door properly, he, too, can be sent to prison. One aspirant who gave an unacceptable reply had to chugalug a huge mug of beer mixed with a sticky syrup. Another was forced to down two glasses of wine simultaneously with one hand. When prisoners are released from prison, they arm themselves with spears, swords, bows, and arrows, and don Tonkinese hats, old képis, and stained solar helmets before parading around the table at the slow Legion pace singing "Eugénie," a song dedicated to the empress of Napoleon III reflecting the Legion's service in Mexico. This incongruous parade continues until the president orders the former prisoners to sit down. Because of these high jinks, some lieutenants get precious little to eat before their plates are whisked away, and the president's departure from the table signals the end of the meal. I suppose the noisy exuberance of the lieutenant's mess helps these young officers let off steam and relax. They are, after all, under considerable pressure in their role as leaders of men in a hard business. But I sat through the performance slightly embarrassed with a fixed grin on my face. I guess age calls the cadence. I was much more at ease on the upper floors.

Strangely enough, despite the sit-down meals I enjoyed with the 2nd REP while at Calvi, I will always remember the sandwich of mustard-smeared garlic sausage in a buttered, crusty roll dispensed as a morning *casse-croûte* by a young Legionnaire as we waited to board a revving Transall. It was a cold morning, the crumbs blew away in the slipstream, and there was nothing with which to wash it down, but it had been delicious.

The paras of the 2nd REP, like other Legionnaires, learn early on that they can depend on the Legion's Department of Morale and Mutual Assistance based at Aubagne. While still on active duty, they can profit from the Department's Leave Center at Malmousque in Marseille, a resort-like seaside complex overlooking the Mediterranean. Later, when pondering retirement and the problems of returning to civilian life, the Legionnaire can seek advice and assistance from the Department and Legion veterans' groups that provide additional support and links with veterans' homes at Strasbourg and Auriol. The largest concentration of retired Legionnaires can be found at Puyloubier.

The town of Puyloubier is located twenty-one kilometers east of Aix-en-Provence in a small, quiet valley. The "Domaine Capitaine Danjou," the Legion's retirement home, is located a short distance from the town among low hills covered by vineyards. Tall, wrought-iron gates open onto a tree-shaded courtyard before a Provençal-style manor that houses the Domaine's principal administrative offices. This is the edge of Cézanne country and the Mont-Saint-Victoire is not far away. Smoke from vineyard clearing fires rises straight into the morning air, and one has an overall impression of tranquillity. But this is not a retirement home where aged pensioners sit indoors staring at flickering television sets. Although some residents have been immobilized by war wounds and old age, most Legionnaires remain active in retirement.

Puyloubier has a working vineyard and farm staffed and worked by the former Legionnaires. It produces the red table wine served at Camp Raffalli and other Legion installations, one that has achieved official classification as a Côte du Rhone. The farmyards are filled with pigs, chickens, guinea hens, geese, ducks, and other animals destined for the mess. At one point during my visit, as I was being shown a low barn filled with plump guinea hens, a former Legionnaire arrived carrying a large carton filled with chicks. He tripped on entering the door, the carton flew into the air, opened, and spewed a multitude of chirping chicks onto the dirt floor where they scattered in all directions like wind-up toys gone mad. The former sergeant in charge of the poultry barn turned the air blue with his curses, but the humor of the situation soon brought a smile to even his lips. In addition to the vineyards and the farms, some retirees work as artisans, producing wood carvings, ceramic souvenirs of the Legion, and leather work to be sold by active Legion posts and to visitors at Puyloubier.

About 180 pensioners, including veterans of the 2nd REP, live at the Domaine Capitaine Danjou, their food, housing, and subsistence provided by the Legion. Some look forward to rare visits from friends or relatives who may travel long distances from their homelands to see their "Legionnaire." Other residents have few, if any, links to the outside world. Their only family remains the Legion. Periodic ceremonies of remembrance at the neatly maintained cemetery of Puyloubier bring decorated former Legionnaires with their flags to lay wreaths in honor of absent comrades. The dead buried at Puyloubier share the cemetery with General Rollet, the "father" of the Legion, another famous Legion officer, Prince Aage of Denmark, and a certain Legionnaire

Zimmerman. All three were exhumed with the Legion left Sidi-bel-Abbès in 1962 and reburied at Puyloubier. Marble plaques fixed to a stone wall at the far end of the cemetery list others who died in past campaigns. The pensioners look forward to these visits, as they liven up the "*popote*" and provide an opportunity for reminiscences and the possibility of a chance meeting with an old acquaintance.

But, like all retirement establishments, the Domaine has its problems. It is not easy for aging men who had previously been so active to settle into a quiet, institutionalized life. Despite the presence of their comrades, there can sometimes be a feeling of personal loneliness and the symptoms of creeping *cafard* (melancholy). In some cases, alcohol presents a problem. The pensioners are technically civilians and cannot be controlled like serving Legionnaires. They can go into town at will and drink in the cafés and bars. Although some effort is made to limit their intake while in the Domaine, the staff cannot serve as enforcers. "Some of these men," a staff member told me, "are among the few who came back; the few who survived Indochina and Algeria. Some of them are *still* in Indochina. They often drink to forget."

10

PROFESSIONALS REQUIRED

France will enter the twenty-first century with an army of professionals.

Jacques Chirac, President of France, speaking
on French Television, February 22, 1996

My final days at Camp Raffalli were spent gathering information I had previously missed and tying up some loose ends. The weather was already improving. The late spring sun was noticeably warmer, and the citizens of Calvi were emerging from their winter hibernation, refurbishing café terraces and slapping new paint on the façades of tourist hotels. One morning a woman's nude body was washed up onto the rocks below the Citadel. From on high, it looked like a pale, discarded doll. A silent crowd watched the *sapeurs-pompiers* (firefighters) gently cover the corpse and carry it to an ambulance, before returning to their daily chores.

My appearances at the camp were now routine, and the paras had learned to live with my presence. Those whom I knew personally stopped for the ritual French handshake; others—aware only of my purpose—greeted me with a quick nod. My appearance at the 3rd Company's "Club" for a beer before lunch hardly caused a stir, but it was frustrating to find my drinks were always paid for by the Legionnaires. When they decide you are a guest, they mean it.

I had spent a little more time in the museum, including a short visit at the same time as several short-clipped, newly assigned officers who had been sent there to absorb a bit of regimental history. They dutifully made their rounds, pausing before certain exhibits and bypassing others. I had intended to ask them a few questions, but the churchlike quiet of the museum and their reverential mien defeated me, so I sought the sunshine. Once outside, I tried to guess which of the newly minted officers had come from Saint Cyr and which from other officer schools, but it was not an easy game. Instead, I reviewed some notes I had taken from a publication on the Legion, listing just a few famous Legionnaires.

The short list would have captured the attention of any Paris socialite or hostess of a cultural salon. Ernst Junger, the German expressionist writer, was a Legionnaire in the 1st Legion Regiment in 1913. Blaise Cendras, French novelist and poet of Swiss origin, served as a corporal in the Legion's Régiment de Marche from 1914 to 1916, losing an arm in combat and winning the *Médaille Militaire*. Louis II, Prince of Monaco, a major general, served as commander of the 1st Legion Regiment between the two world wars. Ali Khan, son of Aga Khan III, was a lieutenant in the 1st and 6th Legion regiments in Syria from 1938 to 1939. Prince Napoléon, pretender to the throne of France, was a simple Legionnaire in the 1st Regiment in 1940. The Hungarian-born writer and philosopher Arthur Koestler served as a Legionnaire in the same regiment the same year. The Count of Paris, pretender to the throne of France, direct descendant of Louis-Philippe I, founder of the Foreign Legion, served in the 1st Regiment under the name of d'Orliac from 1940 to 1944. Hans Hartung, well-known French abstract painter of German origin, was a Legionnaire in the 1st Regiment from 1940 to 1942. Fernand Gravey, a French movie star and director of Belgian descent, was a member of the Legion's Régiment de Marche from 1944 to 1945, and Frederic Rossif, a renowned film director and specialist in nature documentaries, was with the Legion's 13th demibrigade from 1944 to 1948.

My last notes were a potpourri of technical facts. Later, I would have to fax a series of follow-up questions from Ireland to Calvi where a hard-pressed Captain Trotignon, filling in for Major Brottier, responded efficiently within twenty-four hours.

I confirmed that the CRAP is now using the French G-9 parachute during operational drops that allows more lateral drift for navigational purposes; that five 89mm LRAC antitank weapons, each with ten rockets, are found in each combat platoon; and that the RAC 112, a 112mm antitank rocket, can pierce 700 mm of armor at 400 meters distance. I also learned that Saint Michael was adopted as patron saint of all French paras during World War II when a medallion of the saint was struck for the parachutists of the Free French forces in London and used as identification once they had jumped into occupied France.

In addition, I found that the present pay packet of a Legion para provides a definite incentive for joining. With a 40 percent jump bonus, a para private receives 6,000 French francs ($1,200) a month; a corporal, 8,000 French francs ($1,600); and a caporal-chef, 9,000 French francs ($1,800). Considering that the para is housed, fed, clothed, provided with free medical and dental care, and is unlikely to use much of his monthly pay while on overseas operations, it is easy to see the appeal of a five-year hitch as a Legion para. This is particularly true for those recruits emerging from the chaos of central and eastern Europe. By comparison, a nonpara Legion private earns 1,500 francs a month. In his excellent book, *The French Foreign Legion*, Douglas Porch mentions the pre-World War I command wisdom that, "the more Legionnaires were paid, the more they would drink." One of the pensioners at Puyloubier had explained that hazards to be avoided in the old Legion were the gamblers and borrowers. Unwary newcomers often fell into the lending trap and regretted it for the rest of their service, particularly if the borrower turned out to be an ill-tempered noncom. Things have definitely changed since then.

Although these last bits of information were significant, I was more interested in the paras themselves and how they differed from the men I had known in Indochina forty-five years ago. Considering the time gap and the cultural and political changes in the world since the 1950s, such comparisons were hardly fair. Nevertheless, there were some obvious differences. The paras in Vietnam, officers and men, had been involved in a grinding, costly war with no light at the end of their particular dark tunnel. Their only hope and solace had been to concentrate on their daily responsibilities, to do their jobs as well as possible. They were generally older than their modern counterparts, and some of them had seen almost continual combat since their baptism of fire in WWII. Heavy losses, exhaustion, and a growing lack of confidence in the brass who directed them from on high had combined to form a carapace of cynicism and draw them together in an even tighter and more exclusive band of brothers. This was not to say that they were brooding or morose company. On the contrary, well aware of the fleeting quality of time, they had lived their lives with a unique, rough brio—an élan that did not always endear them to the provost marshal's office. The Legion paras of 1952 were concentrating on two prime targets—defeating the enemy and survival. They viewed the future as a smudged mirror that no amount of wiping could clear. Watching the sun rise each day was a bonus.

Today's para lives in a world where the threats of conflict and the risks of combat are no less real, but long, drawn-out wars with doubtful conclusions are less likely. For these men, the mirror is clear, and the paths of the future can be studied and chosen. Some of the corporals and 1st class privates I spoke with impressed me with their ideas on career planning. Those who had decided to stay in the Legion were already anticipating applying for special training courses that could gain them more stripes and push them up the Legion ladder. The aspirations shared by these young men were those of hope and an unspoken but genuine confidence that they had a good chance of surviving their military careers.

Appropriately, the real contrast between then and now came to me one morning in the field, as I watched an antitank team struggling up a steep hill under the weight of their heavy weapon. Shutting my eyes momentarily, I was suddenly back at the Plaine des Jarres in Laos in the early fifties. The sounds were the same: the clank of equipment, the panting, cursing search for a solid foothold, the noncom's voice urging his men on. It all seemed familiar. But, when I opened my eyes, I saw the real difference. The paras I had known on that mournful Laotian plain had been sinewy, hardened veterans with closed faces who rationed their humor like a rare commodity. With a few exceptions, the young Legionnaires climbing that Corsican hill had not yet been tested. Their smiles came easily. How long those smiles will last is an open question.

The average Legionnaire tends toward silence in the face of personal questions, even if his superiors have given him permission to be interviewed. It is not so much that he has dark secrets to hide. It is more likely that he prizes his privacy and does not consider media exposure part of his contract. Nevertheless, my scribbled record of some responses indicates various outlooks.

"I came here to soldier, with soldiers. That's what I'm doing." (English-speaking *caporal-chef.*)

"I'll do my time and retire with a pension as a French citizen while I'm still young." (Private from Eastern Europe.)

"The Legion is special. Everyone knows that. That's why you're here, isn't it?" (Private first class from Belgium.)

"I've never been healthier, and I like being outdoors. The Legion is what I expected, but it takes a while to adjust to the the life." (English-speaking private.)

"Don't believe what they tell you." (Anonymous.)

For today's Legionnaire, the world offers no relief from the plagues of continued limited intensity conflicts, brush wars, ethnic and religious conflicts, and lethal acts of organized terrorism. Events in Bosnia and Chechnya have demonstrated the powderkeg status of the Balkans after the cold war as well as the equally explosive situation in the Caucasus. Western Europeans have awakened with a certain degree of shock to the fact that their continent—even without the threat of the Warsaw Pact—can be a most dangerous environment. The new Africa is riven with ethnic and tribal conflicts nurtured by a system of military dictatorships that make the ancient tribal chiefs appear benevolent by comparison. The Middle East bristles with armament and sputters with hate. An unpredictable China is testing its growing ability to project military and naval power in Asia.

This all contributes to the continued prevalence of violence as a commonplace sociopolitical tool and the necessity of confronting such international threats with determination and the required force. Faced with what amounts to an era of global conflict, the western democracies are attempting to cut defense expenditures and are finding it difficult to recruit men for their defense forces.

Ironically, recruiting may now be the least of France's future worries. On Thursday, February 22, 1996, Jacques Chirac, the president of France, dropped a veritable bombshell with an announcement on national television. He proposed a sweeping new defense program that would provide France with a more efficient defense and a more productive armament industry at a reduced cost. In so doing, the president explained carefully, the defense forces would be reduced considerably and the traditional, compulsory conscription of French youth would be abandoned. Part of this new look would include a reduction in the strength of the Army Ground Forces from two hundred thirty-five thousand to one hundred thirty-five thousand. France's shift to a professional army is to take place over a period of five years.

As expected, this announcement met with opposition from various quarters. The French Left sees any abandonment of conscription as a break with the Republican, citizen-soldier tradition dating from the Revolution—a tradition that tended to bring Frenchmen from all regions together for a period of service under the tricolor. The same critics have hinted that a professional army, under certain circumstances, could post a threat to democratic government. They do not hesitate to recall the Revolt of the Generals during the Algerian War. Some military authorities whose turf is most threatened, however, have not hesitated to go public with their own doubts. Within twenty-four hours of the presidential announcement, a former commander of the French Army's Airmobile Brigade filled a half page in the Paris daily *Le Figaro* with a defense of his former command and a warning of what France would stand to lose if the brigade were dissolved. Other military men and defense officials are expressing the fear that the eighteen thousand men and two hundred forty-two tanks of the 1st French Armored Division in Germany—the prime French contribution to the European Corps now commanded by a French general—will be among those units to suffer retrenchment.

French regions that depend on military installations and defense industries for economic survival are particularly wary of the new plan. At Tarbes in the Hautes-Pyrénées, politicians of all parties are preparing to fight for the retention of the Regiment of Parachute Hussars and the Regiment of Parachute Artillery—over two thousand men—stationed in their town. They are also joining together to preserve the livelihoods of eighteen hundred employees of the local Arsenal where turrets for the LeClerc tank are produced.

Chirac's argument for change was founded on the premise that a massive invasion from the East was unlikely, and large conventional units should no longer consume either resources or the time of strategic and tactical planners. He stated that France does not currently have an army capable of fulfilling

France's political responsibilities and stressed the need for a professional army ready for sudden, limited conflicts abroad. Citing the Gulf War as an example, Chirac pointed out that the professional British Army was able to put forty thousand troops on the ground in the Gulf during a comparatively short time, while the French took months to assemble a force of ten thousand men. "Never again," the president insisted, predicting that, "France will enter the twenty-first century with an army of professionals."

One major military problem that has hampered many French governments would be solved by the new plan. Previously, conscripts in the ranks of French Army units were exempt from overseas service in the world's hot spots. This meant that, during a deployment alert, the gaps left by conscripts in combat units would have to be filled by regulars from other regiments or conscripts who had volunteered for an overseas posting. This was an awkward, impractical state of affairs that automatically involved more delays. Now, those units that survive the purge—and whose ranks will be filled with regulars—will be ready for rapid overseas deployment, depending on the needs of the government.

Judging from the latest deployment figures, the needs of the French government are many and varied. As of March 1996, France had thirty-eight thousand troops operating overseas as follows:

18,214	Germany	1,270	Senegal	576	Ivory Coast
9,228	Former Yugoslavia	1,098	Indian Ocean Zone	324	Pacific Ocean
3,453	Djibouti	840	Chad	247	Lebanon
1,390	Central African Republic	609	Gabon	143	Turkey
131	Saudi Arabia	56	Haiti	30	Niger
30	Western Sahara	20	Angola	16	Sinai
15	Kuwait	10	Cameroon	5	Georgia

These deployments cover troop commitments to international forces such as the NATO Implementation Force (IFOR) and the United Nations; defense treaties with specific countries; training missions, and observer assignments. France has defense agreements with eight former colonies and military assistance agreements with many more African states. One thousand French military advisers are active in twenty-three African states, and two thousand officers from these nations are trained in France.

Where does the Foreign Legion, and particularly the 2nd REP, stand in this period of major change? On the same day that President Chirac unveiled his new defense plan, Joseph Fitchett of the *International Herald Tribune,* writing under the head "Chirac to Unveil Plans for an All-Volunteer French Army," stated, "Currently, France's only all-volunteer unit big enough to operate in a major battle is the Foreign Legion, whose 8,500 men are spread between missions in Africa and Bosnia."

It is too early to speculate on the specific results of the Chirac defense plan, but an editorialist for the *Paris Daily Liberation* summed it up with the word "projection." He explained that it consisted of providing France with an ultra-mobile force of fifty thousand to sixty thousand men—"battle proven professionals, as well trained as they are equipped"—capable of simultaneously conducting two or three lengthy interventions beyond the territory of France. One does not have to be a military expert to realize that the all-volunteer Foreign Legion and its Parachute Regiment provide the perfect working models for this major defense reorganization.

France is not alone in facing new strains within its defense establishment. The British ministry of defense recently declared it was having great difficulty meeting its annual recruiting quota, particularly for the combat arms. Cut to the bone by recent financial restrictions and smarting from the compulsory disbanding of some of its famous regiments, the British Army is now faced with the requirement of sending troops back to Northern Ireland. If the Irish Republican Army rejects attempts to restore the cease-fire and continues to talk about "twenty-five more years of war," the strain on Britain's defense forces will increase. Serving officers mutter darkly about current and future reductions in combat personnel and transport capabilities that will make it impossible ever again to envisage a campaign similar to that in the Falklands. A sign of these lean times was an announcement confirming that the elite Special Air Service (SAS) had accepted its first recruit from the ranks of those classic mercenaries—the Gurkhas.

More and more the question is posed, "Where have all the soldiers gone?" Somewhere along the line, some western military forces seem to have lost a sense of their true mission. The froth generated over the years by recruiting officers who concentrated on the advantages of learning a trade or a specialty in the service tended to obscure the realities of a soldier's calling. Phrased simply, a professional soldier's trade is combat, and combat involves possible death and disablement. Sugar coat this basic fact with ethereal promises, and it is little wonder that many youths shy away from the combat arms, seeking safer billets in service and specialist units. If this trend continues, and a costly operation somewhere in the world produces a heavy casualty list, even a super-power might think twice about further commitment. The American withdrawal from Somalia after the loss of U.S. Rangers in Mogadishu comforted our enemies and planted doubts in the minds of our friends. More and more nations are hesitating to risk their forces in conflicts that do not directly threaten either their own vital interests or their home territory.

Much has been said recently about the eventual organization of a permanent international Rapid Reaction Force. The establishment of such a force depends to some extent on the performance of the NATOIFOR in Bosnia. But, however the Bosnian situation develops—and the seeds of disaster are ever present—a huge effort such as IFOR does not fit the profile of a Rapid Reaction Force. The key word here is "Rapid" and IFOR, for all its firepower and presence, is primarily a one-shot politico-military creation under the banner of NATO. Much can be learned from its deployment, but the fact remains that IFOR is more ponderous than rapid and flexible.

Nor is the model of UNPROFOR, the United Nations Protective Force any longer valid. Despite the dedication and sacrifice of some UN contingents, the Bosnian tragedy cast a merciless light on some hard truths about the effectiveness of UN forces. Such helter-skelter troop mixes have the makings of a field commander's nightmare. Operational misunderstanding, ethnic incompatibility, the need for specific rations, language problems, religious differences, drug and alcohol abuse, and black marketeering are only some of the problems posed by a hastily mustered international force under UN supervision.

With its professional Foreign Legion of 8,500 men and 350 officers, including the 1,350-strong 2nd REP, a member of France's Force d'Action Rapide (FAR), France has been able to respond quickly and efficiently to varied but limited overseas crises without the problems posed by conscripts in the ranks of other French Army units. Thanks in part to the Legion, the demands of international military cooperation and operations such as the Gulf War and Bosnia were met.

Some critics perennially disapprove of the Legion and mumble darkly about "mercenaries." Some influential Frenchmen express lingering doubts about the Legion and its role in a democracy. They are quick to pounce on any media reports of racism, rowdiness, or latent violence to justify their fears. In many such cases, the "Legionnaires" in question are often green recruits traveling by train to Aubagne and their first screening, months way from qualifying for a *képi blanc*, treating their nervousness and adieu to civilian life with too much alcohol and macho bluster.

Webster's *New World Dictionary* straightforwardly defines a mercenary as "a professional soldier serving in a foreign army for pay." Granted, the "dogs of war" that ranged postcolonial Africa gave a new, negative meaning to the word mercenary. Nevertheless, it is time we reevaluated the term. As he struggled to form a viable Continental Army, George Washington welcomed the assistance of French, Polish, and Prussian officer mercenaries. We may be a long way from establishing an international Rapid Reaction Force of varied nationalities, but it is not too early to study such a possibility.

The day before I left Corsica, I stood on the ramparts of the Citadel looking out on the wind-riffled Bay of Calvi. A shiny white ketch was luffing its way toward the harbor entrance, and the roar of Transall engines carried in on the wind. Minutes later, parachutes peppered the sky, descending rapidly toward the water. That evening we ate pork and lentils in the mess and broached an extra bottle of Côte du Rhône to mark my imminent departure.

Later, I took the dark, cobblestoned route into Calvi for a nightcap at "Au Son des Guitares." The cafe was booming with a Saturday night crowd of Legionnaires, the music was loud, and the bar girls were rushed off their feet. Walking in without a escort from the Legion was a mistake. I drew a barrage of suspicious glances as a lone civilian, until a group of three Legionnaires from Camp Raffalli recognized "Monsieur Simpson" and took me under its wing. I was thus finally able to break my status as a "guest of the Legion" and buy a round of drinks. Later, I reclimbed the hill as the church bells struck midnight, pausing only to bid adieu to the unimpressed and indifferent colony of stray cats sheltering within the walls of the Citadel.

The next morning, Major Brottier interrupted his Sunday to drive me to the airport to board a light aircraft for the short, bumpy flight over the Mediterranean to Marseille.

* * *

Putting together the story of an active, fighting parachute regiment in a comparatively short time was sometimes hectic, occasionally frustrating, and always interesting. Some readers may believe I have been too sympathetic in my presentation of the 2nd REP and displayed a pro-Legion bias. Perhaps—but it is not because I am either a propagandist for the Legion or a military romantic. I have experienced three wars, a bloody revolt, and assorted coups, demicoups, and minicoups as a soldier, war correspondent, and Foreign Service officer. Such a background has made me profoundly appreciative of the combat soldiers who perform the dangerous chores assigned to them by their governments—the kind of work that must be done when the chips are down. War is a nasty, stomach-wrenching reality—a constant, alas, of the human condition. My respect for the Legion is based upon the demeanor of its members as true military professionals who approach their difficult and dangerous assignments without bombast or complaint.

On a more personal level, the officers and men I met at Camp Raffalli maintained a reassuring level of good humor that rounded off rough edges and acted as a dissipator of the "petty details" that plague many military units. My time as an enlisted man during World War II provided me with the necessary expertise in detecting that particular curse. The following sample of that wry, perennial humor recently appeared in the *Bulletin of the Foreign Legion Association of the U.S.*

Laws of Combat

of

The French Foreign Legion

1. If you're short of everything but targets, you're in combat.
2. Anything you do can get you shot, including doing nothing.
3. Incoming fire has the right of way.
4. Don't look conspicuous, it draws fire. Corollary: if you look conspicuous, try to look unimportant because the enemy may be low on ammunition.
5. No plan survives the first contact intact.
6. If the attack is really going well, it's an ambush.
7. The enemy diversion you're ignoring is the main attack.
8. The important things are always simple—the simple things are always hard.
9. If the enemy is in range, so are you.
10. Never forget your weapons were made by the lowest bidder.

As an outsider and temporary visitor to the 2nd REP, I also failed to sense any obvious tensions, antagonisms, and serious problems. That is not to say they do not exist. To the trained eye, however, the surface signals were not there. I must admit to one serious frustration. I had hoped to devise a new title for the regiment's *commandos de recherche et d'action dans la profondeur.* For several evenings, I scribbled out possible substitutes without success. The current title may play well in francophone regions, but no proud combat unit should have to go into action with the acronym of CRAP.

I have tried to keep up with the movements of the 2nd REP while writing this book, but there must be a cutoff time. In November 1995, one thousand paras of the 2nd REP returned to Bosnia (the 2nd, 3rd, 4th, 5th companies, along with the CEA and the CCS). At first under UN orders as part of the Rapid Reaction Force, the regiment then joined the IFOR under NATO command and was deployed at Mostar and Mount Igman. Its mission: to "verify" the application of the Dayton Accords concerning the demilitarization of the former front line zones. During February 1996, the regiment turned over these positions to an Italian brigade and moved farther south to the vicinity of Konjic, Borca, and Kalinovik. The 2nd REP's Bosnian assignment ended in April 1996 with the regiment's return to Calvi. The total casualties while in Bosnia were two dead and twenty-two wounded.

On November 27, 1996, a telephone conversation with the *le Chef d'Escadrons* Brunot, director of the Legion's Information Office, informed me that the regiment's 3rd and 4th Companies returned to Chad on October 16 in the ongoing context of operation *Épervier.* One day later the 2nd Company departed Calvi for Libreville, Gabon. These assignments put three combat companies of the 2nd REP within easy deployment range of the Zaire-Rwanda crisis zone if needed.

APPENDIX 1

EQUIVALENT RANKS

French Foreign Legion	U.S. Army
General de Brigade	Brigadier General
Colonel	Colonel
Lt. Colonel	Lt. Colonel
Commandant	Major
Capitaine	Captain
Lieutenant	Lieutenant
Sous-Lieutenant	Second Lieutenant
Aspirant	(no equivalent)
Adjudant-chef	Chief Warrant Officer
Adjudant	Warrant Officer
Sergent-major	First Sergeant
Sergent-Chef	Master Sergeant
Sergent	Sergeant
Caporal-Chef	(no equivalent)
Caporal	Corporal
Soldat de 1re classe	Private First Class
Soldat de 2e classe	Private

Appendix 2

Battles and Battle Deaths

Operations and Battles of the 2nd Foreign Legion
Parachute Regiment

Indochina 1949–1954

Nghia Binh
Nghia Lo
Bavi
RC-6
Phu Doan
Na San
Plaine des Jarres
Lang Son
Dien Bien Phu

Algeria 1955–1967

Collo
El Milia
Tébessa
Djebel Darmoun
Guelma
The Aurès
Bône

Kolwezi 1978

Chad 1969–1970, 1978–1980, 1983–1985

Lebanon 1982

Rwanda 1989–1994

Gulf War 1990–1991

Somalia 1992–1993

Sarajevo 1992–1993

Bosnia 1995–1996

THE REGIMENT'S BATTLE DEATHS

Indochina............	32	Officers
	85	Noncoms
	707	Legionnaires
Algeria.............	9	Officers
	24	Noncoms
	200	Legionnaires
Chad..............	1	Officer
	3	Legionnaires
Zaire..............	1	Noncom
	4	Legionnaires
Djibouti............	1	Officer
	4	Noncoms
	23	Legionnaires
Bosnia (March 1996)....	2	Legionnaires

Reading List

The following books will provide more background on the Foreign Legion to interested readers.

Bergot, Erwin. *La légion au combat*. Paris: Presses de la Cité, 1975.

——. *La légion au combat II*. Paris: Presses de la Cité, 1984.

Bocca, Geoffrey. *La Légion! The French Foreign Legion and the Men Who Made It Glorious*. New York: Thomas Y. Crowell, 1964.

Mattei, Antoine. *Tu suvivras longtemps: Les baroudeurs de la Légion en Indochine*. Paris: Olivier Orban, 1975.

Murray, Simon. *My Five Years in the French Foreign Legion*. New York: Times Books, 1978.

Porch, Douglas. *The French Foreign Legion: A Complete History of the Legendary Fighting Force*. New York: HarperCollins, 1991.

Sergent, Pierre. *Les maréchaux de la Légion*. Paris: Fayard, 1977.

——. *Camerone*. Paris: Fayard, 1980.

Windrow, M. *French Foreign Legion Paratroops*. London: Osprey, 1985.

Young, J. R., and Erwan Bergot. *The French Foreign Legion: The Inside Story of the World Famous Fighting Force*. New York: Thames and Hudson, 1984.

For those who prefer a fictionalized account of the "old Legion," any available reprint of P. C. Wren's *Foreign Legion Omnibus* is recommended. First printed by Grosset & Dunlap in 1928, this volume includes *Beau Geste, Beau Sabreur,* and *Beau Idéal*.

INDEX

About the Author

Howard R. Simpson is a former U. S. consul general, a novelist, and a writer on defense matters. A decorated U. S. Information Agency correspondent, he covered eight major operations during the Franco-Vietminh War. He later served as advisor to the president of the Naval War College and as deputy director of the State Department's East Asia/Pacific Bureau of Public Affairs. Simpson has published thirteen books, including *Dien Bien Phu: The Epic Battle America Forgot* (Brassey's, 1994). His writing has appeared in *Harper's, Commonweal,* the *International Herald Tribune, Newsday, Military Review, Army,* and other publications. He lives in Ireland.